Intermittent Fasting 16/8

The 16:8 Method Step by Step
to Lose weight, eat healthy
and feel better
following this lifestyle

25 Delicious Recipes &
Meal Plan for 4 Weeks

MARK WILLIAM

Legal Disclaimer

The information contained in this book and its contents is
not designed to replace or take the place of any form of
medical or professional advice and is not meant to replace
the need for independent medical, financial, legal or other
professional advice or services, as may be required. The
content and information in this book have been provided
for educational and entertainment purposes only.

The content and information contained in this book have
been compiled from sources deemed reliable, and is
accurate to the best of the Author's knowledge,
information, and belief. However, the Author cannot
guarantee its accuracy and validity and cannot be held
liable for any errors and/or omissions. Further, changes
are periodically made to this book as and when needed.
Where appropriate and/or necessary, you must consult a
professional (including but not limited to your doctor,
attorney, financial advisor, or such other professional
advisor) before using any of the suggested remedies,
techniques, or information in this book.

Upon using the contents and information contained in this book, you agree to hold harmless the Author from and against any damages, costs, and expenses, including any legal fees potentially resulting from the application of any of the information provided by this book. This disclaimer applies to any loss, damages, or injury caused by the use and application, whether directly or indirectly, of any advice or information presented, whether for breach of contract, tort, negligence, personal injury, criminal intent, or under any other cause of action.

You agree to accept all risks of using the information presented inside this book.

You agree that by continuing to read this book, where appropriate and/or necessary, you shall consult a professional (including but not limited to your doctor, attorney, or financial advisor, or such other advisor as needed) before using any of the suggested remedies, techniques, or information in this book.

Table of Contents

Introduction

The world of weight loss and overall health and well-being is a confusing one. It seems that every single week there is a new fad diet on the block or another addition to something which we thought we had mastered the understanding of. Who said being healthy was easy?

For anyone who has weight to lose, it's important to find the right type of diet to suit your needs. In many ways the "right" kind of diet won't be a diet at all, it would be a lifestyle change which helps you lose weight, become healthier, and sustain it all in the end.

It seems that the low carbohydrate, high-fat combination lifestyle change is a popular one at the moment, but that doesn't work for everyone. Having to count carbs, protein, and make sure you're eating enough fat content can be too time-consuming, and it's also not so easy to incorporate this kind of eating regime and general lifestyle change into your routine.

Have you heard of intermittent fasting?

The word "fasting" puts many people off, but this new routine is far easier than you might think, and it actually yields some very beneficial effects for your health; of course, one of those benefits is weight loss.

Intermittent Fasting 16/8

This book is designed for anyone who wants to become healthier, have more energy, turn back the ticking clock of aging, as well as anyone who wants to lose weight and maintain a healthy number on the scales afterward. We'll first talk about what intermittent fasting is, as well as exploring its many benefits. Of course, we want to give you all the information possible, and that means both sides of the coin; in that regard, we'll cover a few of the possible downsides too. If you have all the information available to you, you can make an informed decision as to the best way forward.

If you do an online search into the various different types of intermittent fasting, you'll see a long list of methods. This book isn't going to give you a huge amount of choice and confuse the matter further, it's going to give you the easiest to follow, the easiest to incorporate into your lifestyle, and that is the 16:8 method. We will talk about the other methods just for the sake of completeness, but the 16:8 is certainly the method we would choose if we were going to make a decision.

You'll see why when we get into more detail, but because we need to give you all the facts as responsible information providers, and you're an adult who can make their own decisions, you'll find a chapter dedicated to the other intermittent fasting methods, as well as their pros and cons.

At the end of the book, we'll also give you a bonus chapter, a gift from us to you. This is a compilation of over 20 delicious and easy to make recipes which will easily fit into your new 16:8 lifestyle, whether you choose to make them on a regular basis or not. The idea is that you can see how easy this lifestyle is to follow and how it really doesn't restrict you in any way at all. All you need to do is eat healthier and try new things as a result. That's not so hard, especially when you start to feel the benefits coming your way. Weight loss and general health and well-being have a habit of being quite addictive once you experience them.

If this all sounds a little confusing at this point, don't worry. Everything will become abundantly clear as you make your way through this book, and as your understanding grows. In the meantime, your excitement should grow too!

Chapter 1: Intermittent Fasting

While growing up, you may have been told that you need at least three meals a day (and especially breakfast) to live a healthy life. On the contrary, recent research has discovered that it's better for your body to skip some meals. That's where the concept of intermittent fasting comes in. In its simplest terms, intermittent fasting is a type of fasting that requires you to take a break from eating. It is a conscious decision to skip certain meals. In this case, you must eat, stop, and eat again. In other words, intermittent fasting (commonly referred to as IF) is not really a diet. Instead, it is an eating pattern or a way of scheduling meals in a way that ensures that you get the most out of them. IF does not really change what you eat. Instead, it only changes when you actually eat. When you fast and feast when you want, IF will mean eating calories during a certain window of the day then choosing not to during the rest of the time.

Additionally, this method isn't crazy about cutting your calories or being obsessed about reading labels (although it definitely does help). In fact, when starting out, you just maintain your calorie intake at the level that you are used to. And when you do that, you can be sure that you will derive all the benefits that come with IF (including losing weight, maintaining muscle mass, and getting lean). When you start your journey through intermittent fasting, you will soon realize that it is simple enough that you will actually do it, but meaningful enough that you will actually notice a difference in your life.

So how does it work?

For us to understand how IF works, it is necessary that we start by learning the difference between the fasted and fed state. When we eat, the body goes into a fed state whereby it is digesting and absorbing food. The fed state begins when you start eating and lasts for up to three to five hours when your body digests and absorbs the food that you just ate. In the fed state, it is very hard for the body to burn fat, especially because your insulin levels are quite high (when you eat food, insulin is produced in response to trigger the body cells to start absorbing the food from the bloodstream). At that time, the body's top priority is to use up the nutrients (mainly glucose) in your bloodstream. But as time goes on, the body then goes into a post-absorptive state—a fancy way of saying that the body is not processing food. This state lasts for about eight to 12 hours after your last meal, after which your body then goes into the fasted state. When your body is in the fasted state, it is likely to burn more fat because your insulin levels are quite low. In this state, your body can burn the fat that wasn't accessible during your fed state. Unfortunately, given that it takes about 12 hours after our last meal for our bodies to get into the fasted state, it is very rare for our bodies to get into this state. That's why many of us who start IF will lose fat pretty fast without even changing what we've been eating, how much we eat, and how often we exercise. This is because fasting essentially puts your body into a fat burning state, which you rarely make it to during your normal eating schedule.

Tip: By cutting out an entire meal, you are highly likely to eat more food in your other meals, yet still consume a significant caloric deficit (which is very important if you want to lose weight).

Note: The period that you eat your meals is called the window period. During this period, you get to eat as much food as you need and after the window period, you resume fasting. The type of intermittent fasting that you embark on will determine the number of hours for your window period. I will discuss more on that when I mention the methods of intermittent fasting. What's important for now is to keep in mind that your fasting period should last for up to 14 hours straight for your body to enter strict fasting mode.

I know you have many questions to ask about intermittent fasting such as:

- "Wouldn't my body break down my muscles during the fasting process?"
- "Is there any science that backs intermittent fasting?"
- "Isn't it unhealthy to go for that long without food?"
- "What if I get very hungry during my fasting period?"
- "Is there any danger to it?"
- "Am I fit for intermittent fasting?"

There is no need to worry. You will receive answers to all your questions as you read. Let us take it a step further by examining some of the health benefits you can derive from intermittent fasting.

Chapter 2: Ways to Fast Intermittently

In order to be successful, consistent, and regular while fasting intermittently, you need to find a method that can fit into your lifestyle. Here are six popular ways to go about it.

1.   16:8 Method

This method is so popular that the next chapter of this book is dedicated to explaining how to use it to get started. Basically, it entails not eating for 16 hours each day of your fast and then having an eight-hour window in which you can eat two to three meals. During the fasting period, it is fine to drink water or beverages that are non-caloric like tea or coffee. Simply do not eat anything after dinner, and by the time lunch rolls around the next day, it will probably have been around 16 hours. If you are someone that naturally skips breakfast, you may find it easy to adopt this method, also known as the "Leangains protocol." Many health experts recommend that women change the regime slightly and eat after 14-15 hours because they tend to do better with a slightly shorter fast. In order for this to be an effective weight loss method, it is important that you eat healthy meals during your eight-hour non-fasting window and not processed or refined foods. Many people find it easy to adjust to this method of intermittent fasting and it becomes effortless to them. Pros of this method, among others: it saves money because you are eating fewer meals, you do not have to count calories, and it burns fat. A difficulty with this method is that it is very strict about what you can and cannot eat. It is good for people who consider themselves gym addicts and endurance athletes. Martin Berkhan developed this method.

2. Eat-Stop-Eat

In order to pull this off, you do a complete 24-hour fast either once or twice a week. The best way to accomplish this is to go from the end of a meal to the same meal-time the following day. An example is if you finish dinner at 7:00 p.m. on a Saturday, you would not eat again until 7:00 p.m. on Sunday. You can also go from breakfast to breakfast or from lunch to lunch, whatever is more convenient for your lifestyle. Again, water and any other non-caloric beverages are fine. Eat normally during the periods of eating, but aim for healthy foods over junk. You may find it too hard to go 24 hours right away and need to build up over time, starting with 15-16 hours at first and working your way from there. This method takes a lot of self-discipline, but it may be preferable if you want to eat normally most of the week and focus your fasting to just a day or two. Pros of this method include that it requires less willpower because you know that your fast is short. You can also somewhat eat what you want as long as it is in moderation. Brad Pilon is credited with creating this method of intermittent fasting.

3.   The 5:2 Method/Diet

This method is very similar to Eat-Stop-Eat but does not require you to fast for a full 24 hours. To do this method, eat normally for five days a week and restrict yourself to 500-600 calories per day twice a week. Some studies suggest women are supposed to aim for 500 calories and men for 600. This is usually broken up into two small meals for the day. The two low-calorie counting days in which you somewhat fast should not be consecutive. This method has had the least amount of research done and critics are quick to point out that there are no scientific studies showing its effectiveness, therefore it cannot be recommend. Plus, this method does require you to keep track of the calories you are eating, so that's a disadvantage.

4.   The Warrior Method/Diet

Fast all day, and then feast at night if you want to try this. This kind of reminds me, and perhaps you too, of the Viking movies where the warriors come back to the lodge and there are baskets and plates of abundant food waiting. During the day, you are allowed to snack on fruits and vegetables, as long as they are raw. Then at night, you eat one giant meal. You technically get a four-hour window to eat at night, but most users of this method stick to one large meal. This method of fasting/dieting agrees with the paleo diet in which people try to stick to healthy, natural, unprocessed foods that resemble foods found in nature. Of all the diets to become popular in recent years, the warrior diet was the first to involve a type of intermittent fasting. Pros of this method are: 1) You can eat appropriate snacks. 2) It is very, very healthy. The con is that you have to really monitor yourself and make sure you are making healthy food choices. Other than raw fruit and veggies, you are fasting for a full 20 hours every day. This method is credited to Ori Hofmekler. There are some similarities to the Ramadan or the 30-day Muslim fast, with Ramadan being mostly spiritually motivated.

5.   Alternate Day Fasting

If you are up to the challenge, you can try to fast every other day. This is an extreme method that should not be attempted by beginners, but you can choose to go with a full-on fast or to limit your calorie intake to about 500 every other day. Many of the scientific studies that showed the health benefits of intermittent fasting used a sort of alternate-day fasting. Ideally, while using this method, you are still eating at least once a day, with your fast going from dinnertime to dinnertime every other day. The pros of this type of fasting are: 1) You will experience rapid weight loss, with people averaging a one to two-pound drop per week. 2) It requires less will power for you eat a little on fasting days and you can look forward to eating more the next day. The con is that you have to be very, very careful to not binge on your eating days. Dr. James Johnson created this type of intermittent fasting when he realized it is clearly impossible for most working people to maintain a consistent calorie restriction by pure will power.

6.   Meal Skipping

You do not need to follow an incredibly strict schedule to get some benefits from intermittent fasting. Today's market-oriented forces have convinced the majority of us that we need to eat every few hours or we will start losing muscle tone and begin to starve. If you are not feeling hungry or are too busy to stop and eat, simply skip a meal. Simply doing that actually has some benefits. Generally speaking, and discomfort aside, the human body is configured in advance to handle up to famine, so skipping a meal or two will not cause you any damage. Skipping a meal or two when it works out best for you is basically a spontaneous intermittent fast done in a very natural way. Just make sure that when you are eating, it is healthy food.

No matter what method of intermittent fasting you chose, it is important to reiterate the following: remember to make good choices when picking your foods. It will not matter how long you fasted if you are gorging yourself on junk food during your eating periods.

There's another far less common method of intermittent fasting known as the "fast/feast" model, but I do not recommend it. In this regime, you eat whatever you want for a full 24 hours and then you fast for a full 36-hours. You then repeat the cycle for some time. It has been known to promote rapid weight loss. However, most people do not want to fast for that long, and they tend to "cheat" to such an extreme that the fast is therefore ineffective.

Chapter 3: The 16:8 Method Step-by-Step

Now it's time to get into the real nitty-gritty of what this method actually entails.

We've mentioned that there are many different types of intermittent fasting and some do actually ask you to fast for 24 hours a few times a week. The 16:8 method differs because there are no long and arduous fasts, you simply fast for 16 hours every day, and eat normally for eight hours.

Now, 16 hours may sound like a lot, but you are going to be asleep for most of it. You see, you can move the fasting period to suit your needs. We'll talk about how to follow the method in more detail shortly, but a good example is someone who needs to eat breakfast versus someone who doesn't want to eat early in the mornings. We're all different, but most of us fall into one of these two categories. You might wake up starving and need breakfast otherwise you can't focus, or you might wake up and simply need a coffee and feel a little sick if you eat straight away.

There are two ways you can manage this, just to give you an example of what the 16:8 method looks like.

If you need breakfast, you can eat it as soon as you wake up, kick starting your eight-hour eating period. So if you wake up at 8:00 a.m., you have breakfast at 8:30 a.m. and that means you need to finish eating by 4:30 p.m. You might go to bed at 10:00 p.m., which means you're only consciously fasting 5.5 hours. As you can see, it's not as horrendous as it sounds, and you can drink water, non-calorie containing drinks, and unsweetened black tea or coffee during your fasting times too. It's actually highly recommended that you drink plenty of water anyway, because dehydration is not something you want to play Russian roulette with.

The other scenario is that you are someone who doesn't really want to eat when they wake up. In this case, you can get up, get dressed, have a black, unsweetened coffee, and you can skip breakfast, starting your eating window at lunchtime. So for instance, you would begin eating at 12:00 p.m. This means you can eat freely until 8:00 p.m. You would then perhaps sleep at 10:00 p.m., which means you're effectively not consciously fasting very much. This is why the 16:8 method is so popular.

Of course, during your eight-hour eating window, you need to be mindful of what you're eating. If you cram those eight hours full of chips and chocolate, then you're going to eat far more calories than you should in the full 24 hours of the day, and you'll probably gain weight rather than lose it! If, however, you're mindful of what you eat, not particularly being restrictive, but simply thinking more along the lines of health, you'll be full and satisfied by the end of your eating window and ready for your fast. This means you will lose weight quite easily and receive the overall benefits of intermittent fasting too.

Can you see how easy it can be? You might wonder if you are actually going to be able to obtain the main benefits we discussed in our last chapter if you're not really putting yourself under a huge strain, i.e. not fasting for days straight. But the answer is yes! You are still fasting, you're just doing it subconsciously for the most part. This doesn't matter in terms of the benefits, because they'll still come your way—fasting is fasting.

1. Best for Beginners

The 16:8 method is one of the easiest to follow and easiest to understand, which is why many beginners choose it. Of course, it doesn't suit everyone and because one size doesn't fit all, it might be that some people switch to a different method after a short amount of time. That's fine, and that might be something you want to think about. We're going to cover some alternative methods a little later, so always bear in mind that if you find the 16:8 method isn't working as well as you want it to for you, then there are other alternatives.

For the most part, however, the 16:8 or Leangains method is very successful for many, and it is a method which encourages healthy eating without rules and regulations in terms of restriction. There are no massive changes to lifestyle, which is something which many people struggle with when they try a different eating routine like the keto, Atkins, or paleo diets. These all come with a lot of rules and regulations, and there are lists of what you can and can't eat, and how it should be prepared. This can overwhelm many a beginner and cause them to rebel against it and say no thanks! The 16:8 method and many other intermittent fasting methods don't come with those rules attached. There is no weighing or counting required, simply making healthy decisions, which aren't rocket science. For example:

• Pizza is bad, brown bread is better.

• Chocolate is bad, fruit is better.

• Cake is bad, vegetables are good.

Can you see how easy it is? Making healthy choices is not complicated and it doesn't mean you have to be 100% healthy all the time. Want a burger? Have one, but only once a week, and make sure the rest of that day is packed with healthy foods.

The other plus point is that the 16:8 method doesn't have to affect your social life. Most people want to head out with friends or their partner for dinner on occasion, or perhaps out for a few drinks, but this can be very difficult when following a low calorie or fad diet. With the 16:8 method, all you need to do is ensure that you schedule the get-together for your eating window. This might be more difficult if you're starting your eating window early and finishing early, but you can always meet up for lunch instead of dinner. There aren't restrictions on what you can eat, but in most restaurants, you can always make healthy choices on the regular menu. If your eating window finishes a little later, that means you have more scope in terms of time.

Let's sum up the main reasons why most beginners opt for the 16:8 method:

21

• It's easy to follow and doesn't require any counting, weighing, or monitoring.

• You can alter your eating time according to your needs.

• You can set much of your fasting period into your sleeping period, so you don't notice it quite so much.

• This eating method doesn't need to interfere with your social life much at all.

• You are not restricted on what you can eat, provided you make sensible, generally healthy choices.

• It doesn't feel like a diet, it feels more like a new lifestyle with timing, rather than food you can and can't eat.

• You can still have calorie-free drinks, water, and unsweetened, black tea or coffee.

• You won't notice hunger quite so much with this type of eating plan, as there are no extremely long fasts involved.

2. How to Follow the 16:8 Method

The 16:8 method is very flexible, and that means you can choose your own specific eight-hour eating window, according to your day. You might work shifts, and that means you sleep at different times. What you should do in that case is pick an eight-hour window which is when you are mostly awake.

Intermittent Fasting 16/8

For example, if you are working nights and you are sleeping between the hours of 10:00 a.m. and 6:00 p.m., you can eat from 6:00 p.m. until 2:00 a.m. You would then probably be working until the following morning when you would head off to sleep, but you could drink coffee (unsweetened and black) to keep you going also, and plenty of water. This might not work for you, so you could think about shifting your pattern and starting it later, perhaps if you don't feel like eating the moment you open your eyes. You could then choose an eating window of 9:00 p.m. and eat freely until 5:00 a.m. It's really up to you.

We've already covered the two main methods most people try with the 16:8, and that is skipping breakfast and starting to eat at lunchtime routine, or in the case of someone who really needs breakfast because they can't concentrate without it, eating earlier and starting the fast eight hours afterwards.

It's not only about when you can eat, but it's also about what you eat too. Whilst there are no restrictions and no lists of foods you must eat and foods you shouldn't, always remember that if you suddenly pile a huge breakfast or lunch on your plate after fasting, you're going to end up with stomach ache. That could mean that you end up eating too many calories within your eating window and actually put weight on, or you end up with stomach disturbances for the rest of your eating window, don't get enough fuel during that time because your stomach is so bloated you can't bear to eat, and then you're hungry during your fasting time. It's about choosing carefully, which we'll talk about a little more shortly.

Intermittent Fasting 16/8

So how many calories should you eat? It depends on whether you want to lose weight or maintain. A standard calorie amount to maintain weight is 2,500 calories per day for a man and 2,000 calories per day for a woman. This does depend on the height, current weight, and metabolism of the person, and is really only an average, healthy amount. If you want more solid guidelines on your specific circumstances, speak to your doctor, who will be able to give you a calorie plan tailored to your needs.

Within that calorie amount, you should make sure that you get a good, varied diet. That means proteins, carbs, fats, vitamins, and minerals. Again, we're going to cover what you can and can't eat loosely because there are no rules, but varied is the way to go. Ironically this will also help you enjoy your new lifestyle more, because you're not bored and eating the same things all the time. This is a pitfall many people suffer from regular low-calorie diets; the change is so restrictive that they end up eating the same thing day in, day out, and over time they get so bored and simply rebel against it. This usually ends in a binge day which causes extreme guilt and then leads them to give up on the diet and go back to eating whatever they want.

While following the 16:8 method, you should also make sure that you drink plenty of water throughout the day, whether fasting or eating. This ensures that you don't become dehydrated and will also aid in digestion. In addition, you should also exercise.

Now, there are no rules to say that you must exercise while following an intermittent fasting routine, but it will help you lose weight faster, and it will help with your general health and well-being. Exercise is fantastic on so many levels, not least helping to build lean muscle, which also boosts your ability to burn fat as an energy source. Exercise is also known to help with mental health issues, such as anxiety and depression, as well as stress. We all live stressful lives, and a little exercise can sometimes be enough to reduce it to levels which are extremely manageable. Aside from anything else, exercise can be a sociable and fun activity.

So, let's quickly sum up how to follow the 16:8 method.

• Eat for eight hours a day, consecutively—you cannot break these hours up, they must be observed as one block of time.

• Fast for 16 hours per day. Again, this needs to be done consecutively.

• You can choose when you use your eight-hour eating block, but it's a good idea to stick to the same times every day so your body gets into a routine.

• Your fasting times should coincide with sleeping to cut down on the amount of conscious fasting.

• Do not be afraid to miss breakfast. In this eating routine, there is no "important meal of the day," there is simply an important eating window.

• You can drink unsweetened black tea and coffee, water, and other non-calorie drinks freely throughout your eating and fasting times, and you should certainly consume enough water throughout the day to ensure you don't become dehydrated.

• During your eating period, you should spread your meals out carefully, so you don't "binge" when you initially break your fast. This will only lead to stomach aches and other unpleasant gastric symptoms.

• Choose healthy meals as much as possible, but there are no restrictions on what you can eat. If you go unhealthy, however, remember that you're not going to create the calorie deficit required for weight loss.

• While you don't need to count calories when following the 16:8 method, it's worth bearing the standard calorie amounts in mind, which is 2,500 for a man and 2,000 for a woman, as a daily average.

• You should also exercise if you want to gain extra health benefits and speed up weight loss.

• Never be tempted to cut down your eating window or to restrict your calorie amount beneath the average. This will lead you towards extreme hunger and also borderline starvation if you refuse to eat. Remember, fasting is not starving!

3. What You Can and Can't Eat

Again, there are no rules on what you can eat and what you can't eat, it's a totally free choice when following the

Intermittent Fasting 16/8

16:8 diet. What you should bear in mind however is overall health and choices which are considered healthy, compared to unhealthy.

The idea is to create that calorie deficit during the full 24-hour span. You do this by ensuring that you fast and eat for the correct ratios of time, e.g. eight hours eating and 16 hours fasting, and that during your eating times you stick to healthy options as much as possible. You will feel infinitely better as a result.

If you want a few ideas on some of the healthiest foods you can incorporate into your day, check out the list below.

• Eggs - Make sure you eat the yolk because this contains the vitamins and protein.

• Leafy greens - We're talking about things like spinach, collards, kale, and Swiss chard to name a few, and these are packed with fiber and are low in calories.

• Oily and fatty fish, such as salmon - Salmon is a fish which will keep you feeling full, but it's also high in Omega-3 fatty acids which are ideal for boosting brain health, reducing inflammation, and generally helping with weight loss too. If salmon isn't your bag, try mackerel, trout, herring, and sardines instead.

• Cruciferous vegetables - In this case, you need to look to Brussels sprouts, broccoli, cabbage, and cauliflower. Again, these types of vegetables contain a high fiber, which helps you feel fuller for longer, but also have cancer-fighting attributes.

Intermittent Fasting 16/8

• Lean meats - Stick to beef and chicken for the best options, but make sure that you go for the leanest cuts possible. You'll get a good protein boost here, but you can also make all manner of delicious dishes with both types of meat.

• Boiled potatoes - You might think that potatoes are bad for you and in most cases they are, especially if you fry them, but boiled potatoes are actually a good choice, particularly if you're lacking in potassium. They are also very filling.

• Tuna - This is a different type of fish to the oily fish we mentioned earlier and it's very low fat but high in protein. Go for tuna canned in water and not oil for the healthiest option. Pile it onto a jacket potato for a delicious and healthy meal.

• Beans and other types of legumes - These are the staple of any healthy diet and are super filling too. We're talking about things like kidney beans, lentils, and black beans here, and they're high in fiber and protein.

• Cottage cheese - If you're a cheese fan, there's no reason to deny yourself, but most cheeses are quite high in fat. In that case, why not opt for cottage cheese instead? This is high in protein and quite filling, but low in calories.

• Avocados - The fad food of the moment is actually very healthy and great for boosting your brain power. Mash it up on some toast for a great breakfast packed with potassium and plenty of fiber.

• Nuts - Instead of snacking on chocolate and chips, why

not snack on nuts? You'll get great amounts of healthy fats, as well as fiber and protein, and they're filling too. But don't eat too many, as they can be high in calories if you overindulge.

• Whole grains - Everyone knows that whole grains are packed with fiber and therefore keep you fuller for longer, so this is the ideal choice for anyone who is trying intermittent fasting. Try quinoa, brown rice, and oats to get you started.

• Fruits - Not all fruits are healthy, but they're certainly a better option than junk food. You'll also get a plethora of different vitamins and minerals, as well as a boost of antioxidants into your diet, ideal for your immune system.

• Seeds - Again, just like nuts, seeds make a great snack, and they can be sprinkled on many foods, such as yogurt and porridge. Try chia seeds for a high fiber treat, while being low calorie at the same time.

• Coconut oil and extra virgin olive oil - You will no doubt have heard of the wonders of coconut oil, and this is a very healthy oil to try cooking with. Coconut oil is made up of something called medium chain triglycerides, and while you might panic at the word triglycerides, these are actually the healthy kind. If you want to go for something totally low in calories, you can't beat extra virgin olive oil.

• Yogurt - Perfect for a gut health boost, yogurt is your friend because it will keep you full and it also has probiotic content, provided you go for products which say "live and active cultures" on the label. Avoid both the sugary yogurt treats and anything that says "low fat." Normally, this isn't as positive as it sounds.

There are plenty of delicious foods to try here and you can easily create some tasty recipes with any of those ingredients. We'll share some recipes a little later in the book, so you can see how easy and satisfying healthy eating can be.

So, what shouldn't you eat? There is nothing that is off limits, but it's about how much of it you eat. If you want a slice of pizza, you can have a slice of pizza, but make sure you only have one and that you have a healthier diet for the rest of the day. Remember, one of the reasons why intermittent fasting is so popular is because it doesn't wag its finger at you when you grab a chocolate bar once in a while. You don't have to feel guilty because you gave in to a burger craving once a week, provided you know that moderation is the key.

What is moderation exactly? It's knowing when to stop and knowing what is enough and what is too much. For instance, enjoying pizza in moderation could mean having a couple of slices of pizza once a week. You still get to enjoy what you like, but you don't have it all the time. Similarly, moderation is stopping at two glasses of wine, rather than drinking the bottle. It basically means you still get what you want, but you don't go overboard.

The key is to exercise while fasted, keeping your body in a ketogenic state, so you are burning more fat for fuel than sugars.

No matter what type of diet you are trying, losing weight is a matter of "calories in" versus "calories out." (To lose weight, you must ingest fewer calories than your body uses for all of its functions during a given time window.) The interesting thing about eating in an eight-hour window is: there is only so much that you can eat before you feel full. This means it is important to eat according to your expected energy expenditure and activity levels. Below is an example of a menu you can use to start out the 16:8 Intermittent Fast.

My best recommendations for your eating window of eight hours depends on your exercise training schedule or on your regular schedule, if you don't exercise routinely. Typically, I recommend that you fast from 8:00 p.m. to 12:00 p.m. the next day. This gives you between 12:00 p.m. to 8:00 p.m. to eat. During your fasting time, I recommend you consume only liquids and natural plant-based sweeteners.

From an exercise standpoint, try to fast through the time when you normally exercise. While you fast, you can exercise in the morning right when you wake up, or just before lunchtime. The key is to exercise while fasted, keeping your body in a ketogenic state so you are burning fat for fuel rather than sugars or simple carbohydrates.

Here is an example of a ketogenic diet plan for this method of fasting:

Day 1

Wake-Up: You can have coffee, tea (non-caloric, without sugar), or water, whichever you choose.

Intermittent Fasting 16/8

Morning: Again, stick to liquids like water, coffee, and tea, and zero-calorie natural sweeteners like stevia or xylitol.

Lunch: Chicken breast with lots of leafy green vegetables or another protein source like meat, pork, fish, or turkey. Try to add some good fats like coconut or avocado.

Snacks: Nuts and seeds are great snacks during the day.

Dinner: Have dinner between 6:00 to 8:00 p.m. Salmon (or another healthy fish or protein source) with vegetables.

Bedtime: Try to stop eating two hours before you go to sleep.

Day 2

Wake-Up: Same as day one, coffee or tea (non-caloric) to get you moving as needed.

Morning: Stick to the same liquids as Day 1. Again, go for natural sweeteners, not artificial ones.

Lunch: Protein with vegetables.

Snacks: Nuts, seeds, or berries.

Dinner: Same two-hour window for eating one or two small meals. Try baked chicken breast with oven-roasted vegetables.

Bedtime: Always try to wait two hours after you eat to go to sleep.

Your diet will want to contain mainly unprocessed foods. Meat, fish, eggs, vegetables, and just a small amount of low glycemic fruit is what your meals should consist of mostly. Processed foods tend to be very high in calories while being very low in nutritional value. If you feel you need a "cheat day," try to save that for the weekends.

Drink lots and lots of water. Try to drink at least ½ an ounce per day for every pound of your body weight. (For instance, a 130 lb. person would drink about two quarts per day, and about three quarts for someone weighing 190 lbs.) This seems like a lot of water but the reality is this will help keep you full and hydrated. The average person typically thinks they are feeling hungry when actually they are just feeling thirsty. Drinking water will help suppress feelings of hunger. You can also chew sugar-free gum to give your mouth something to do (and producing saliva). Studies have shown that some gums have certain sweeteners that turn into calories in your stomach, so make sure you are sticking to the sugar-free variety.

Traditionally, most exercise trainers and coaches have recommended eating a big breakfast or four to five balanced meals throughout the day. The 16:8 method skips breakfast as an extension of the natural overnight fast.

It is a good idea to use your fasting time to be productive. Sitting around and feeling hungry will only make things harder on yourself moving forward.

The 16:8 method is often used in combination with a strict exercise regime and as such should be used in combination with branch chain amino acids. How and when to use them will be discussed in the next chapter.

Also, if you are coupling your 16:8 intermittent fasting

with an intense workout regime, it is recommended that you add more protein to your evening meal. Look for animal or plant-based proteins, or a protein supplement.

Chapter 4: The Benefits of 16:8 Intermittent Fasting for Your Health

Intermittent fasting techniques, including the 16:8 method, are most commonly used to assist in weight loss by the general population. The method has been tried by thousands of people and also scientifically proven to be a helpful resource in reducing body fat and improving body composition. In fact, weight loss is often considered the number one reason why people opt for a diet and program that utilizes intermittent fasting.

While a reduction in body fat is definitely one of the best advantages to be mentioned in terms of intermittent fasting, there are more advantages that people gain when they decide that they are going to follow this type of program—especially if they truly commit to it and can implement self-control that ensures they do not give in to cravings.

Intermittent fasting is known to assist in improving your body composition as well, as I mentioned earlier. Body composition refers to a series of features—this includes your body fat percentage and lean muscle mass, primarily. A program that utilizes intermittent fasting, along with an appropriate diet plan, will bring down your body fat percentage and push up your lean muscle mass at the same time.

It is also important to note the benefits that are associated with weight loss for people with an excessive amount of fat distributed throughout their body. Since excess weight and obesity is linked to so many chronic diseases that can truly make your life dreadful, losing even small amounts of weight can drastically reduce your risk of these diseases. Additionally, if you have already been diagnosed with a disease associated with obesity, reduced body weight may improve the symptoms that you are experiencing and help you get the disease under control.

Take type 2 diabetes, for example. In one study, scientists describe that factors such as pro-inflammatory markers, cytokines, hormones, glycerol, and non-esterified fatty acids are all increased among people who are obese. In turn, these factors all have factors that link them to insulin resistance. When insulin resistance develops, it can continue to progress into type 2 diabetes if the affected person does not implement appropriate preventative measures.

When you develop type 2 diabetes, you become predisposed to many additional risks and complications. In fact, type 2 diabetes can cause severe complications that may not only lead to disability but also become life-threatening. This disease can also affect all of the body's most important organs, including the heart, and can damage various tissues, such as nerves, throughout the body.

In addition to assisting in reducing body weight and bringing down the risks associated with obesity, intermittent fasting has many other benefits that are also worth mentioning.

Through intermittent fasting, cellular changes may occur in the body. This can lead to levels of human growth hormones rising by as much as 500%. This leads to a faster rate of fat burning, while also producing an increase in muscle mass.

It has also been found that intermittent fasting can help to remove waste that has built up in cells within the human body and can also assist in the repair process of cells that have been damaged. This means cells in the body become more efficient in performing their specialized functions.

One study also explains how recent findings from scientists suggest that intermittent fasting helps to improve brain health and may play a crucial role in helping medical experts better understand how diseases like Parkinson's and Alzheimer's can be prevented in the future.

Furthermore, following an intermittent fasting plan can also help to reduce levels of inflammation within the human body, as well as help to fight against oxidative stress. Both of these factors are known to significantly contribute to numerous chronic diseases and can cause certain molecules to become damaged, which can inhibit their functionality within the body.

In one study, scientists tested how intermittent fasting would work on brain health and cardiovascular health among a group of laboratory rats. They found significant improvements in various tests used to determine the well-being of these two crucial hormones in the body. The scientists also associated these improvements among the tested laboratory rats with the reduction in oxidative stress that was observed. Additionally, the scientists also observed an improvement in the cellular stress resistance ratings in these rats. What this means is that an intermittent fasting diet can help to reduce the effect that stress has on the body and help to fight against the existing oxidative damage, often also referred to as free radical damage, that has already occurred.

Chapter 5: The Potential Downsides of Intermittent Fasting

Everything in life has pros and cons, and because we believe in being transparent and complete, allowing you to make a decision that is based on all of the information and not just some of it, it's important to point out the possible downsides of intermittent fasting too.

The biggest downside of intermittent fasting is that you do need to fast for some of the days in order to make it work. That is the deal. The good thing about the 16:8 method, as you will come to find out, is that you can easily stretch that to ensure that you're sleeping for most of it, so it is far less noticeable. You can also move your fasting period to the times which suit you. It doesn't matter when you fast, provided you follow the rules and fast for the right amount of time consecutively.

Of course, fasting will make you hungry at first. This is also something you can't avoid. Over time, the non-hungry plus point will kick in, but at first, you're likely to notice pangs. These might also be quite severe in the beginning, but you will find ways to deal with them, such as distraction techniques, delayed gratification, and drinking water. Much of the time when we think we're hungry we're actually not; we're normally just bored or even thirsty. Taking a drink of water or even having a cup of unsweetened black coffee or tea is allowed during your fasting periods, and this can take the edge off any hunger pangs you're feeling.

The biggest challenge that most people face when starting the intermittent fasting lifestyle is not overeating during their eating window. When you've been fasting for x number of hours, you're going to be hungry by the time your eating window starts. This can mean that you're quite open to grabbing the biggest meal around, no matter what it contains. Remember, intermittent fasting doesn't tell you what you can and cannot eat, but you do still need to eat healthily. There is no diet on this planet that will let you eat chips, pizza, chocolate, and all the sugary, carb-laden treats you normally crave because these are inevitable causes of weight gain. You can have the odd treat when following intermittent fasting, but the willpower you need to develop stops you from overindulging when your fast finishes.

You will probably also come to quickly realize that if you overindulge after a fast, your stomach is going to tell you very loudly and possibly quite spectacularly that it doesn't approve. Having a heavy meal after a fast can lead to stomachache, gas, and upsets. It's best to stick with light foods and build up over time. Developing willpower and knowing the difference between healthy foods and terrible foods will be something you learn quite quickly, but the fact that nothing is restricted can often mean those with less self-discipline can fall foul of this biggest of intermittent fasting pitfalls.

There are also a few concerns about women finding it harder to complete intermittent fasting, compared to men. This is all down to hormones. Women are far more sensitive to calorie fluctuations than men because women have different hormones. This means that when calories are restricted, hormone levels change. When hormone levels change, side effects can occur. The good news is that the 16:8 method we're discussing is one of the best intermittent fasting methods for women because it doesn't affect hormones to a great degree. Some other methods that ask you to fast for a full day a few times per week, are far more likely to cause hormonal disturbances for women. For the most part, you can manage any side effects by choosing the right method.

Pitfalls of Intermittent Fasting and How to Avoid Them

You have poor nutrition habits

I mentioned this briefly already, but it bears repeating; you can't eat garbage all the time. Like anything else in life, you will get out of intermittent fasting what you put in. If you want to lose weight by intermittent fasting, you will have more success and faster results by eating healthy foods. It is beyond the scope of this book to go into all the details of what healthy foods look like, but we all have some idea of what that means. Eat less processed foods and more "whole" foods. If you have to take your food out of a wrapper or a box, it's a good bet you are eating processed foods. This, of course, takes more time to prepare and plan, but if you are eating less food, you need to make the food you are eating count for your body. Intermittent fasting is not a free pass to eat anything you want. Avoid this pitfall with planning. It is hard to plan meals sometimes, but it is the best thing you can do so you don't end up eating a fast-food burger or microwaving something that resembles food to eat.

You are overenthusiastic

Who wouldn't be excited about all the benefits that can come from intermittent fasting? The problem from all that enthusiasm can mean you jump into the deep end without learning to swim yet. Your body has adapted to a normal rhythm of eating. When you disrupt that, your body will tell you. The more you disrupt it, the more aggressive your body will be at getting the point across that you are messing with its rhythm. Hunger pangs, headaches, dizziness, irritability, weakness, and malaise are just a few of the symptoms you will get when your body is telling you that you are off schedule if you do too much too soon. Avoiding all this is as simple as taking it slow from the beginning, as hard as that may be when you are excited. You will give your body time to adapt to the new rhythm of eating and learn what feels normal for you while you are fasting so you know when something isn't right and you need to dial it back.

All you think about is food and how hungry you are

For most of us, it has been a long time since we were really hungry before starting an intermittent fast. When we start to learn what real hunger is, it's hard not to constantly think about food and how hungry we are. It is a process that everyone goes through. No matter how strong-willed you may be, you will be hungry and you will think about food a lot at the outset. This is normal and most people get over it without too much grief. In the beginning, it can be overwhelming though, and cause you to be unable to complete whatever intermittent fasting method you have chosen. The best way to avoid this is to keep yourself busy. Do the things you love doing to keep your mind off of food. I recommend getting out of the house to do this because it's always easy to go grab food when you are home, and you may already have a habit of snacking while you are watching TV or doing your hobbies. Try to avoid the things you would normally eat snacks while doing.

You fast too long

The whole idea with intermittent fasting is that you do it in short amounts. While there is research to suggest the occasional long-term fast is good for you, you shouldn't do this repetitively. "More is better" is not the motto here. Intermittent fasting stresses your body. These mild stressors are a good thing, so long as you give ample time to recover. Like weight lifting, you can't expect to continue to see better results if you don't give yourself time to recover. When you over-stress your body by doing longer fasts and not giving enough time for recovery, you will see diminishing returns and start to do more harm than good. If you stick with intermittent fasting long enough, you will be tempted to push the limits on these plans because you see results and your body can handle it physically and mentally. The way to avoid this is to recognize that the methods outlined in this book are tried and true and were designed the way they are for a reason. None of the methods call for fasting for more than a day at a time. While there is flexibility to adapt each method to fit your needs, recognize that there are limitations to the stress you can put your body through before it is no longer beneficial.

You abuse coffee

Many people who do intermittent fasting rely too heavily on coffee to bridge the gap between meals. Coffee is great for doing this, but be careful not to become a coffee addict. Caffeine is a stimulant and you can easily become addicted to it if you are abusing it to get you through. If you are drinking coffee throughout the day because you are too hungry, then you probably did too much too soon. I won't deny that coffee is a life saver, but you shouldn't depend on it to complete your fast. Caffeine has a six-hour half-life in the body. This means that six hours after you drink a cup of coffee, it is still having half the effect it did on you when first you drank it. Twelve hours after you drink it, coffee still has ¼ its potency. With this in mind, it's easy to see why you should limit the amount of coffee you drink and how late in the day you drink it. This can dramatically affect sleep cycles and overall health. Since the idea here is to lose weight and become healthier, it is best to keep coffee consumption in check. You can avoid running into problems with coffee abuse by limiting the number of cups you drink a day to one or two, and making sure you don't drink coffee past noon. We all have those days where we need a little extra energy to get through, but it should not be a habit to drink coffee in excess or in the afternoon.

You don't drink enough water

While drinking tea or coffee in the morning when fasting is encouraged to help you feel less hungry throughout the day, this is not enough liquid. The body needs extra water while fasting for several reasons. The first is that it helps you to feel more full by putting something in your stomach. It is also needed because while your body is not focusing its energy on digesting food all day; it is breaking down cells and creating new ones. This expedited healing process leads to an unusual amount of cellular waste that needs to be removed. Adequate hydration allows the body to make this process as efficient as possible. Besides removing cellular waste, the body is breaking down fat stores for energy during a fasting period. Many times the toxins we encounter on a day-to-day basis accumulate in our fat stores, and when we break fat cells down we get an extra strong dose of these stored up toxins. It is vitally important to be well-hydrated when this happens so those toxins are removed from the body and not redeposited somewhere else to cause any harm. Many times when people are experiencing light-headedness and headaches during a fast, it's the result of toxins in their bloodstream that need to be removed. To avoid this, you need to focus on drinking plenty of water while you are fasting. At a minimum, you should be drinking about two liters (or eight glasses) of water every day on your fasting days. Even if you aren't a water drinker, you should start. Try just sipping on water throughout the day if you need to. You will appreciate not getting headaches from your fast.

You are always afraid of hunger

This is worth mentioning again because it is hard to overcome in the beginning. Casual hunger is normal and healthy for the body to endure. You can go weeks without eating food, as long as you drink enough water. The hunger you feel over the hours or day of fasting is manageable and will get better with time. If you are working up to a more rigorous method of fasting, don't let the fear of being hungry hold you back. It will pass and you will survive. The benefits of intermittent fasting are too great to allow casual hunger to keep you from your goals. You can avoid allowing this fear from becoming overwhelming and control it by starting out slow and gradually increasing the time you spend fasting. Your body will not eat itself from the inside out while fasting. It just takes practice to build that tolerance to casual hunger.

You eat too much right before bed

It goes without saying that your meals after a fast will be bigger than normal and if you are ending your fast at dinnertime, you will eat a big dinner. The problem here is that eating a very large meal just before bedtime can disrupt sleep. There are a couple of reasons for this. The first is that when your body is hard at work digesting a big meal, it can increase your body temperature and make you uncomfortable while you are lying there under the covers trying to get to sleep. Digestion causes an exothermic reaction. This means that the reaction among the acids in your stomach and the food you've eaten gives off heat. The more food there is to react with, the more heat is given off. The rise in body temperature subsides as food in your stomach is removed during the digestive process. Beyond being too warm at bedtime, if you eat a big meal of carbohydrates before bed, your body will release a lot of insulin into the blood. This insulin can reduce the effect of the burst of growth hormones that are released during the first half of your sleep cycle. This impairs the healing process and leaves you feeling more tired the next day. To avoid this, try to eat at least three or four hours before you go to bed to give your body time to digest the food and allow you to have a good night's sleep. Intermittent fasting should improve your sleep, as long as you don't eat too close to bedtime.

You focus on the details and ignore the big picture

You will probably do this at some point and have to remind yourself to stop. If you are wondering if a splash of cream in your coffee will ruin your fast, or if cutting your fast short by 15 minutes will ruin your fast, then you are looking at the small picture. You have narrowed your focus too much and need to broaden your view of intermittent fasting again. It is important to remember that the whole is greater than the sum of its parts. The timing of your fast is one part, the food you eat while not fasting is a part, your exercise routine is a part, and when you eat is a part. You have to look at the overall picture and decide if everything together is working for you. Don't hold a microscope to your timing and ignore every other part of the process. Avoid narrowing your view too much and confusing yourself with questions that are really inconsequential to the big picture by focusing on the main things. Focus on what method of intermittent fasting you will use and make sure your average meal contains quality foods. If you do this, it will help keep you from getting lost in the details. It is okay to be detail-oriented, but not at the expense of neglecting all the other parts of the machine.

You are a social eater

One of the hardest things people who fast intermittently face is not hunger, but social situations where people typically eat. If you go to lunch with co-workers regularly and start a fast that entails skipping lunch, it can be difficult. Lunch isn't the only thing you miss, but social interaction with your colleagues as well, which poses an issue when you start your fast. Either you have to remove yourself from the daily lunches and lose that social interaction that most people look forward to in the middle of the workday, or sit there sipping on water while everyone else eats. There are a lot of situations most of us find ourselves in throughout the week where we eat socially and it would be "weird" for us not to. Whether it is with family, friends, or co-workers, there is usually something more than just hunger driving us to eat many of our meals.

To overcome this situation, there are a lot of things you

can do. You can avoid the situation altogether and just not participate in social settings where people will be eating. You can excuse yourself from eating by telling people you just ate or come up with some other reasonable excuse or you can tell people you are familiar with what you are doing so they understand why you aren't eating, but be prepared for all the comments they may make to convince you that you are doing something unhealthy. Whatever you choose will be best for you, you have to learn to stand up for yourself and do what is best for you no matter what people say or feel about it. If you like to eat socially, then plan around your fast so you can do so. You will be surprised at how often you get offered cookies at work or get invited to something where people will be eating, once you start fasting. We rarely think about how much it happens and sticking to your fast will bring your awareness to this and help you cut out those excess calories from social eating.

You think that intermittent fasting is magic

It is easy to look at all the benefits of intermittent fasting and conclude that it is magic. The reality is that we are still working within the confines of physiology even if we are optimizing the process. This is not a magic cure for weight loss. It still takes time and effort on your part, albeit less time and effort than many other weight loss methods. You will get results if you stick with intermittent fasting, but it won't be overnight. Intermittent fasting is an amazing way to lose weight and improve your overall health, so get excited, just remember that it is a process limited by your body and has no magic to go beyond what the body is capable of doing.

Chapter 6: Preparing for a Lifestyle Change

How to Start (Setting up Fasting and Feeding Times)

To get started, all you need is a good idea of your daily routine and schedule, as each day is not created equal. Think back and jot down the time frame in which you estimate you do most of your eating on an average day. Next, jot down the time in which you think you get the most sleep. Lastly, jot down other important time frames that are important to your average daily routine. Some important time frames I jotted down and considered initially were happy hours with my spouse and friends, and family dinner time, in which we eat dinner together each day.

I considered that on average, my eating times ranged from 10:00 a.m. to about 8:00 p.m. on weekdays and from 12:00 p.m. to midnight on the weekends, as I have a great social life. With terrible sleeping habits, I was sleeping around midnight, waking up at 8:00 a.m. at the latest on weekdays, and from 2:00 a.m. to 12:00 p.m. on weekends.

Review your notes and decide on the best eight hours out of your day to be considered your meal window. With this schedule, I would say a good starting window would be 12:00 p.m. to 8:00 p.m. daily. With this feeding window, the fasting window would automatically be starting daily at 8:00 p.m. and fast until 12:00 p.m. Some people consume three meals during this eight-hour window, but I found that to be impossible for me, so I consume two moderately portioned meals and eat snacks at other times during the feeding window. You can decide to eat how many meals and snacks you want while intermittent fasting, but make a decision and be consistent.

Meal planning

Meal planning, also known as meal prep, is NOT required to be successful with intermittent fasting; however, it does a good job of preparing you for even more success with your feeding window. Meal prep is preparing some or all meals/snacks in advance to have on hand when needed. This saves you time, so you aren't preparing meals/snacks each day, and it takes away the thought process of what you will eat during your daily windows. By meal prepping, there is less room for failure, especially for beginners. With meal planning comes the bonus of preparing healthier options to eat during your feeding window, instead of choosing quickly processed and prepacked options because it's convenient.

For me, there are many steps to meal planning. This consists of creating full meals (including recipes), creating all-inclusive grocery lists, reviewing your own kitchen to see what you already have and what you need, then altering your grocery list, and finally going grocery shopping.

Designing meals takes creativity. With the internet, there are plenty of recipes and meal ideas for available options. Being creative means not always eating the same thing day in and day out. Change up your breakfast options, lunch options, dinner options, and snacks. Season the food differently. Cook a different cut of the beef. Garnish it differently. Make it a soup or salad instead of a casserole. Make vegetables a snack in some way. Find ways to increase your protein intake. Add more green leaves to your protein shakes and/or more vegetables or fruits. Decide on two to three lunch and dinner options, and two to three snack options.

Once you have decided on what meals you have created and their recipes, you will need to search through your kitchen cabinets, freezer, pantry, and refrigerator to see what you have already and don't need to purchase when you go food shopping. This includes everything: meats, sides, fresh vegetables, fresh fruit, drinks, snack options, spices, herbs, oils, bread, wraps, and more. Revise your grocery shopping list to include what you need.

Go to the grocery store and pick up the items on your list in preparation for meal prep. Meal prep is taking all of your groceries and cutting up everything that needs to be chopped, washing everything that needs to be washed, marinating everything that needs to be marinated, seasoning everything that needs to be seasoned, baking everything that needs to be baked, cooking everything that needs to be cooked, measure everything that needs to be measured to the appropriate portion, and packing it all in individual meal containers to easily grab and go when needed. Although highly recommended, meal planning and prep is NOT required for intermittent fasting.

Intermittent Fasting 16/8

Portion control, food labels, and measurements

Portion control is NOT necessarily required during intermittent fasting; however, because you are not restricting any food groups and you can technically eat what you want during your meal window, portion control becomes even more important than meal prep, but could also work in speeding up the weight loss when treated equally. Portion control does not mean you have to eat tiny portions of everything. Portion control is the serving size on the label or the amount that is generally served. To best practice portion control with your meal prep, measure your foods and package them into the containers before storing them away for later meals. Another tip to ensure you are eating proportionately, is to drink a glass of water to confirm you are hungry and not just thirsty, and to make sure you do not overeat.

Food labels display the ingredient content, nutritional facts, calories, and serving sizes for packaged foods. Reading food labels will ensure you are not eating too much at one time. This is fundamentally portion control at its best. The first thing to review is the serving size. Serving size is the portion size that is generally served at once. The calorie count displays how many calories are in one serving. Food labels also include total fats, cholesterol, sodium, and total carbohydrates per serving size. Additionally, the % daily value displays how much this serving will count towards your daily intake; try not to go over 100% in any category. Reading and understanding food labels are NOT required to be successful while intermittent fasting, but this could enhance results.

Counting net carbs is another big topic of discussion that people tend to gravitate to. To count net carbs, subtract the dietary fiber from the total carbohydrate count, this equals net carbs. Counting net carbs is an acceptable way to eat and meal plan BUT counting net carbs are not required for intermittent fasting.

Measuring foods is NOT necessarily required when intermittent fasting, but it ensures you are not eating too much of whatever you choose to eat. Use smaller containers to ensure you are eating a good amount of food to be full, but not stuffed. Never eat from the package that the snack comes in, and limit distractions while you eat, as people usually overeat while doing activities, such as watching television. Measuring food is important for portion control, but not required for intermittent fasting.

Choose balanced food options wisely

When following an intermittent fasting lifestyle, you are not restricted to any food group and you can choose your own meal options BUT food choices are still (as always) important. It is important to have good nutrition that emphasizes a diet that provides a complete source of minerals, vitamins, and nutrients for the healthiest functioning body.

A diet is considered the sum of all foods eaten, but it refers to the use of a specific intake of nutrition. Any healthy diet should include more whole and unprocessed foods over processed and/or liquid foods to include plenty of fruits and vegetables, lean proteins, some fats and oils, and grains. This would be considered a balanced meal as these are also called energy-dense foods. Energy-dense foods are high in fiber and help to retain natural water.

When fasting, try to eat more non-starchy vegetables and lean proteins. Choose foods that are whole-grain and stay away from refined grains and flours. Fruit is going to be the best option for trying to curb an existing sweet tooth, especially for beginners. Choose non-dairy over dairy, eat fats and oils in moderation, and choose the healthiest forms of fats and oils.

Fresh fruits and vegetables are favored over frozen and canned, but any vegetable is better than no vegetables at all. Choose lean cuts of protein, and to increase your protein intake, add vegetarian sources like beans and soy products. Try almond, soy, or cashew non-dairy options to limit your dairy intake, as dairy is one of the world's leading allergens. Other leading allergens include eggs, peanuts, and shellfish. Make carbs toppers instead of the base of your meals. When buying pasta, bread, crackers, and more, always look for a whole grain listed as the first ingredient on the nutrition label. Eat half of an avocado at least once a day to increase your healthy fat intake.

According to the USDA, there are five principle guidelines to follow to satisfy your dietary needs. Follow a healthy eating pattern across your entire lifespan. A lot of people are not following this first guideline. An eating pattern is your liquid and food intake and your routine way of eating. Following this first guideline ensures nutrient adequacy, healthy body systems, and lower risks to chronic disease invasions of your body. The second and fourth guidelines focus on the amount of food and liquid you consume, how you should eat nutrient-dense foods from all the major food groups, and how to shift from bad choices to good choices. The decisions you make are the most important. You are the important link that makes the difference, you are in control of ensuring you are meeting these guidelines. Meeting these guidelines is everyone's responsibility.

The third guideline is to limit the number of calories that do not come from nutrient-dense foods, such as added sugars, high sodium, and trans and saturated fats. According to the USDA, healthy meals consist of whole fruit, fresh vegetables, dairy, protein, whole grains, and oils. The fifth guideline teaches you how to share your knowledge with others. It states that support is necessary for change for everyone, and that it is on all of us to support healthy eating habits.

Physical activity

Like meal planning, measuring foods, reading food labels, and portion control, exercise is NOT required, but beneficial to your overall results while intermittent fasting. The American Heart Association recommends some form of physical activity for at least 30 minutes daily.

Create a workout schedule. Make a leg day, an arm day, a cardio day, a total body weight day, and more. A schedule starts to make you more consistent and accountable. On days when you feel unmotivated to do one, you have the other. If you are already exercising, intermittent fasting can only improve your results. The combination of intermittent fasting and exercise maximizes weight loss and/or weight maintenance.

Mindset

The biggest barrier will be your mindset. This is made up of the already set attitudes and assumptions you have in your head, specifically as they relate to the relationship you have with food and eating food. Think mind over matter. You matter the most to yourself, so take better care of yourself. To sustain an intermittent lifestyle, you will need to erase or ignore all prior assumptions or attitudes related to diet, lifestyle changes, losing weight, current food habits, current eating schedules, change in general, and more. Once started, try to make optimal choices for yourself and be disciplined in being consistent in carrying out your plans. To be successful, you will need to think and act differently for optimal results.

Surviving longer while hungry

Hunger is feeling uncomfortable and/or weak due to a lack of food. Hunger can be physical, but it can also just be a desire or want rather than a need right at that moment. The body sometimes responds as if it is hungry, but sometimes we are thirsty and are yearning for liquids and not food, so your water intake is imperative to your success in extending to longer fasting windows.

To habituate longer fasting windows and/or to resist food

during your fasting window to make it to the feeding window, staying productive is vital. Stay busy by any means necessary. It is a great idea to exercise during this time or stay busy with your professional or personal work. Being lazy and feeling bored lead to false indicators to your body that you may be hungry, when really you are just in a slump or bored. The more you think about food, the weaker your body thinks your mind is, and eventually this will be your downfall.

Chapter 7: Hacks to Success

There are many principal tips and tricks that I still use to this day to continue to ensure my success. While intermittent fasting is all about the timing of your meals and fasting, it can be so much more if you decide to use all the resources available to you to keep it exciting, continue to learn new things, be creative, be consistent, and be prepared always. Intermittent fasting along with the hacks discussed below will change your weight and your life forever.

Sharing is caring

I am not certain if this will help anyone other than myself, but it did help and is still helping me. I have learned that I'm better everything in life when I am helping others along the way. I have been sharing my knowledge with people day in and day out, and have become an intermittent fasting coach to many. By encouraging others, I have simultaneously helped myself, because it's a shame to teach what you can't follow, right? I won't be that type of coach; I practice what teach. Me writing this book has helped me understand that I know so much about this topic, which is why I have been so much more successful this time around.

I gain so much pleasure from my social media followers' interest in my story and growth. I have so much respect from my coworkers and friends, and they all ask so many questions about IF. Literally, this is all I talk about, which is fine by me, it holds me accountable. I don't want to let myself or anyone else down. When I am helping someone else with this knowledge, it helps me as well.

Apps to download

Pinterest is such a good resource to use when it comes to planning meals to keep eating healthier. This app includes links to recipes, grocery lists, meal ideas, how to prep these meals, and more. YouTube, of course, is a great resource to review other people's struggles, peaks and pits, before and after pictures, and to hear their stories. It can help you stay motivated and understand that most of what you go through while attempting to make this a habit is true for others who have gone through the same things. MyFitnessPal's blog and the community sections of its app is another great resource to use to join communities that are specific to intermittent fasting and all its components.

These are good apps to download onto your mobile device, iPad, or tablet. Using free time on these apps should be your new hobby instead of scrolling on your social media, especially since everything you see and hear will contribute to the success of making intermittent fasting your new lifestyle.

Food delivery services

Some people decide that meal planning and meal prep is just not a realistic lifestyle for them. They may live a busier life than average, have a big active family, hate to cook, can't cook, don't want to cook, hate shopping, not feel creative, and more reasons. These people may choose to use a meal planning/prep or food delivery service to assist them with their meals.

Sometimes this can be costly, sometimes it may be affordable, but it is convenient, and by using this service you are still preparing in advance for what life throws at you during this change. You are still choosing healthier options and being creative with what you eat.

Journaling

This lifestyle change will change you forever. One day you will have changed so much that you may want to share your journey with others. If you decide to share, what better way than to go back and see how you felt each day? It is a best practice to journal while you go through this journey. Journaling can be helpful in discovering what your negative triggers are, tracking your weight and measurement progress, tracking your feelings towards food, tracking your growth toward meal planning, food shopping, eating out, food options, tracking your every step along the way. Your first journal entry should note why you are doing IF and explain your goals.

Sometimes people go as far as to go back to school to study nutrition or to be a trainer, life coach, and more. This journal will only assist you in tracking it all in real time and could be the road to success for others who feel like you once felt. This can also help you when you have those hard days and want to give up. You can go back and read, knowing that you've felt like this before and overcame it, so you can surely do it again. Journaling can only help you on this journey; it's a best practice for success.

Family lifestyle change

I wouldn't recommend making a drastic change, but after a few days or maybe a week, it's a good idea that your family or even the company you keep start eating what you eat and when you eat. If you are the cook and shopper in your house, this will be a better use of your time. You will only have to meal plan once, shop once, and cook a few meals that will feed everyone for a couple of days. Hopefully, this gives you more time during the week to add in exercise if you don't already or add a second workout, or maybe give you a few hours of time each day to do something else you have been wanting to do, like write a book.

Brush your teeth earlier

Everyone should brush their teeth before bed each night. With intermittent fasting, it's better to practice brushing your teeth after your last meal. The taste of toothpaste should keep you from wanting to do any further eating. This is just a mind trick, but it's a successful and helpful trick that I still use.

How to order at restaurants

Know the menu before you go. I repeat, know the menu before you go. Most restaurants, even fast food restaurants, have websites where you can view their menu options. If you know what's on the menu before you go, you can be proactive in deciding what you will order as the best option for you. Have a few staple times that most restaurants offer: grilled salmon, chicken breast, shrimp, seafood, chicken wings with no breading or sauce, burgers wrapped in lettuce, salads, and more.

Most restaurants DO NOT serve appropriate portions of food. This is an advertising mechanism for them and an effective way for them to get you to continually come back and spend money with them. I mean, who wants to go to a restaurant that serves those small plated portions? Most restaurants serve two and sometimes three times the portion that a person should be eating in one sitting.

To ensure you spend your money wisely but get the food you pay for while simultaneously ensuring that you are using good portion control, it' a good practice to go ahead and ask for a to-go box, and when your food arrives, split your food up and keep an appropriate portion to eat now and package away the other two or three servings for later.

Lunch bag prep

Every evening after dinner, clean the kitchen and prepare for the next day. This includes preparing your lunch bag for the next day. I add the following to my lunch each day:

two full meals, three to four snacks, and two to three bottles of water or sparkling water. Although most days I eat dinner at home, what if I don't make it home in time to eat dinner? Or what if football practice goes long? What if traffic is a mess due to an accident? What if I have to work late? What if, what if, what if? Always be prepared and you will be successful. I have had unplanned events that have forced me to eat in the car, and sometimes dinner is only a few healthy snacks because I didn't have my meal with me. Be prepared.

How to deal with unplanned events

Although unplanned life events occur sometimes three to four times a week, as an intermittent faster you still need to have a plan for the unexpected. Always have that lunch bag with you, as previously mentioned. Know a few staple food options that are your go-to choices when you are on the go and don't have your own available food options. Think before you eat, always.

Peer pressure is real, especially at social events. Be sure to have a serious conversation with family and friends so they know you are committed and that they should not offer you food outside of your feeding window. Your new lifestyle is not a joking matter and you would appreciate they accept it as an important part of your life. Make good decisions and be proud of those decisions that you make. Every now and then, I change my feeding windows for social events. I sometimes fast longer so that I can push my feeding window back to be able to attend social events and have dinner and drinks with family and friends.

Buy in bulk

You may be wondering, how is buying in bulk related to intermittent fasting? It is vital for beginners and sometimes long-time intermittent fasters to always have food on hand to accommodate any cravings and their feeding windows. It is best practice to buy favorite snack foods in bulk, if available. When you buy these items in bulk you can then use small ziplock and/or sandwich bags to create your own individual serving size (according to the food label) baggies to keep in your car, purse, backpack, at school, at work, in your gym bag, in your lunch box or bag, etc.

It saves you money to buy in bulk rather than individual items already prepackaged. Companies charge more for convenience, so when you buy prepackaged, small, cute individually packaged items, it costs more than buying in bulk and doing this yourself. This also ensures that you are only having a serving or two according to the food label. This also saves you from not being unprepared and eating unplanned food items.

Consistent routine

Appetite is trainable because it is driven by routine. Our bodies know and learn our routines, we are usually hungry when we expect to be hungry, not necessarily when we are physically hungry. Again, it could be that we are bored or need fluids. Practice makes perfect, right? Fasting is a skill and with intermittent fasting you are advancing this skill.

Intermittent Fasting 16/8

A best practice would be to start with a good routine in your new life as you undertake this lifestyle change. This means set your alarm and wake up to start most days at the same time, specifically during the week. Eat your first meal and a second meal at the daily same times (you can have your snacks at whatever time during the feeding window). It is also a best practice to workout at the same time of the day most days and take measurements, pictures, and weigh yourself on these same days. Meal plan the week before you shop and cook the meals. Then shop on the same day, and cook and prep the meals on the same day, so you always start the week with good habits.

Chapter 8: Losing Weight and Burning Fat

Most weight loss diets are complex and have many rules. It is fortunate that one of the most popular fasting methods to lose weight doesn't have too many rules or conditions. Intermittent fasting keeps it simple—it is a dieting pattern where you tactically skip one or more meals for a particular period.

Intermittent fasting is not about cutting calories from your meal but instead skipping an entire meal. This is why it is considered as one of the easiest dieting patterns. The reasons behind the growing popularity of intermittent fasting are:

- Simple eating pattern
- Effectiveness to lose belly fat and reduce weight
- Other health benefits

Intermittent fasting and weight loss

Intermittent fasting, as the name suggests, is a dieting pattern where you have to fast for a specific period in a day. The fasting usually lasts between 16 to 20 hours, and you eat during the other four to eight hours of the day. The fasting period is referred to as the fasting window and the time you eat is known as the feeding window. During the fasting window (the period you fast), you are allowed to have fluids (water, black coffee, herbal tea, etc.).

You can see better results when you spend more time

fasting on a daily basis. There is no specific chart—you can fast as frequently as you prefer. The more you fast, the more effective the result.

When you follow intermittent fasting, you gain more health benefits apart from weight loss. How does your body lose weight when you fast? Your body uses the stored body fat (nutritional reserve) for energy. This results in burning all the unwanted calories. When you burn calories in this way, you lose weight and also burn the excess fat. This will help you get a lean physique, and you will also feel healthy and energetic, as the body uses the excess body fat (stored fat) for energy. This is because it doesn't get energy from the food intake since your food intake is restricted.

Intermittent fasting helps your body to optimize the release of the major fat burning hormones – especially insulin and HGH (human growth hormone) – the two most important ones. Human growth hormone is responsible for switching on your body's fat burning system. Your body starts to burn all the excess fat to give you the energy to carry on with your regular work routine.

Studies show that fasting increases the production of the human growth hormone (HGH) by 2,000 percent in men and 1,300 percent in women.

Intermittent fasting also has a major influence on the other important hormone: insulin. It helps to keep insulin levels steady and low, which is key to losing excess weight or avoiding extra fat from becoming accumulated in the body. Foods rich in processed carbohydrates and simple sugars accumulate more body fat. It is therefore advisable to avoid these foods as it causes the insulin levels to skyrocket and then crash whenever you eat them. This will result in excess fat accumulation in your body instead of burning it as energy.

When your insulin levels rise, you end up with health issues like obesity, type II diabetes, and various other chronic health conditions. Intermittent fasting is the solution to all of these problems. Clinical studies have proven that 15 days of consistent intermittent fasting helps to balance insulin levels. Your body stays in a fat burning state, giving you more energy all through the day.

Strategies of Intermittent Fasting

Intermittent fasting naturally reduces calorie intake

For a weight loss diet to work, there should be an overall reduction in the total calorie intake. The process of burning more calories than you actually consume is referred to as a caloric deficit. A caloric deficit will lead to weight loss. Intermittent fasting does this naturally.

When you skip an entire meal, you don't take in any calories for that period. This, of course, means that you don't have to worry about the calories when you eat. For instance, when you skip your regular breakfast of lemon juice and toasted sandwiches, you might save about 400-500 calories each day. Now, let's say you are planning to reduce 1,500 calories per day. You have already saved 33% of the calories right away by skipping a meal.

Even if you eat two large meals (600 calories each) after skipping breakfast, you only consume 1,200 calories, which is not too high.

Intermittent fasting helps lose extra fat

When you say you want to lose weight, you essentially mean that you want to lose your body fat. The fact is nobody wants to lose their muscle mass or water content. But most weight loss diets do this: first they cut the carbs and then pull out the water from the body. Ultimately, this weight loss regimen doesn't serve any actual purpose.

Research has shown that fasting helps the body to lose more fat content and less water or muscle mass. On the contrary, most of the other weight loss diet patterns do the opposite. The study was able to prove that intermittent fasting helped people reduce four to seven percent of their waist size in a period of 24 weeks, i.e., they lost belly fat— the most difficult fat to burn in the body.

More studies proved that alternate day fasting (a type of intermittent fasting) reduced around 3.8 kg body fat on average.

Intermittent fasting helps maintain muscle mass

The main problem with most weight loss patterns is that you tend to lose both fat and muscle. To experience healthy weight loss, it is important to maintain the muscle mass of your body. This is because muscle maintenance is fundamental for making sure the metabolic rate of your body doesn't go down too low.

Intermittent Fasting 16/8

If you don't maintain muscle and concentrate only on fat loss, then you might get back the lost fat once you stop the diet pattern. A review shows that overweight people can lose body fat and maintain muscle through fasting as compared to the usual calorie-restriction diets. There was another study which showed that around 25% of the lost weight was muscle mass in the usual calorie-restriction diets. While intermittent fasting (which involved calorie restrictions), only 10% of muscle mass was lost.

Nevertheless, a good protein diet and strength training are the two most important aspects of building muscle mass.

Intermittent fasting works well when your weight gain is at the highest

You don't gain weight overnight, it is a gradual process that happens over the years. Though there is no consistency in the amount of weight we gain, it usually skyrockets during holiday breaks like Christmas and Thanksgiving. Research shows that around 50% of weight gain happens between November and January in a year. So if you keep checking on your weight during the festive seasons every year, you don't need to worry about weight gain. Unfortunately, it is not easy to do, as you might look like a fool when you count your calories and macronutrients during your Christmas feast. But there is a better way! You can observe intermittent fasting during such occasions. For instance, you can skip your breakfast and have a sumptuous Christmas lunch followed by a light dinner.

Intermittent Fasting 16/8

The basic thing here is to miss one or two meals on the day you are planning to feast. This way, you don't really need to worry about missing out on your favorite foods.

Intermittent fasting doesn't give you hunger pangs or yo-yo effects

What is the yo-yo effect? The yo-yo effect, also called weight cycling, is the recurring gain and loss of weight over time. When you introduce your body to a restrictive diet, it causes a shift in your hunger hormones. Due to this, you might end up with uncontrollable food cravings and severe hunger pangs.

Intermittent fasting will not cause the yo-yo effect, as the fasting and eating pattern is broken into intervals. This means such a fasting method can cut calories from your body without making you feel hungry.

Intermittent fasting can be a game changer for you if you:

- Want to lose belly fat
- Can skip meals without making a fuss
- Want to spend less time cooking and cleaning

How effective is intermittent fasting to lose fat?

Intermittent fasting encourages your body to burn more fat. Your blood sugar rises after you finish your meal. The blood sugar and the glycogen (stored carbs) in your body is the energy (your body burns), which is responsible for keeping you alive and functioning in good health. So when you don't eat anything for a longer period, your body's blood sugar and the stored carbs go down. When this happens, your body has no choice but to begin burning the stored body fat for energy.

Your body fat is nothing but the accumulation of all the excess calories that get stored in the body every time you overeat.

The body takes all these excess calories and stores them as body fat (nutritional reserve) to use as a backup energy source when:

- You become calorie-deficient due to heavy exercising or when you eat less.
- Your body is forced to burn all these excess calories, which are stored as body fat, as there are not enough carbs or blood sugar to burn when you are fasting for more than 14 hours.

So when your body fat gets burned for energy, you naturally start to lose weight as all the excess calories are getting burned.

When you combine intermittent fasting with a proper exercise plan, you tend to lose more fat and body weight, thereby giving you a lean physique.

You lose fat faster when you:

- Fast for 14 to 20 hours per day.
- Eat less during your weight loss diet pattern.
- Combine exercising and fasting.

Intermittent Fasting 16/8

Your metabolic rate increases when you observe intermittent fasting. This is because when your energy levels go down, along with your blood sugar levels, your body counter-reacts by releasing more adrenaline (norepinephrine). This gives you more energy and keeps you focused on your regular work routine. Since your body releases adrenaline, it forces your body to burn all the accumulated fat to provide you with energy. These stored fats are mostly found in the hips, belly, and thighs.

It is true that intermittent fasting usually targets the belly fat area. It is extremely difficult to lose belly fat because the abdominal region has more alpha-2 receptors (they slow down fat burning) than the beta-2 receptors (they speed up fat burning). When you observe intermittent fasting, your insulin level goes down, which closes down the A2 receptors (as they can't work well without insulin). This will activate the B2 receptors in your abdominal region, allowing your body to burn the excess fat in the belly. The increased blood flow to the belly area makes it easier for the fat-burning hormones to do their job well.

It is possible to reduce the last bit of fat your body has accumulated through intermittent fasting. And this fasting method is more essential for women, as they have more fat (or A2 receptors) in their thighs, butt, and hips. As mentioned earlier, the growth hormone naturally increases due to intermittent fasting and helps burn more fat. This also stops you from eating more calories, since you skip one or more meals and reduce the calorie intake.

Chapter 9: Getting the Most Out of Exercise

This chapter will give us an opportunity to remind ourselves of the value of exercise, and we will consider the types of exercise that are particularly beneficial to a program of intermittent fasting.

The benefits of exercise

Whenever we can burn more calories than we consume, not only will we be losing weight, but we will be lowering our body fat composition. Hello, six-pack! Fasting is clearly one of the best ways to keep our calorie intake low, but the best way to supercharge this and get the full range of benefits is by combining it with an exercise program.

First, for adults (ages 19-64) we are given a choice to some extent. Whichever route you take, there should be a couple of sessions per week to work on strength exercises to keep your muscles in shape. This is going to very much complement an intermittent fasting routine since we know that will improve our lean body mass. On top of that should be either two and a half hours of moderate aerobic activity (which includes exercise such as cycling or walking briskly) per week, or half that amount of time in vigorous exercise. Jogging fits this category as does, for the more competitively minded, a game of singles tennis.

That minimum activity will help maintain your weight if your calorie intake is about average. It will also support our bodies as we seek to improve heart health, organ well-being, and so on. So for those of us fasting, this will mean weight loss-because our calorie intake will be lower than average.

A brisk walk on weekends and every other day during the week is going to help us lose weight. That really is not a huge commitment. Two forty-minute trips to the gym will offer us the same benefits. However, there is one small caveat to this. While such exercise regimes as mentioned above will ensure we meet our minimum targets for good health, some daily activity is also necessary. This does not have to be severe and can be broken down into 10-minute chunks. A bit of time gardening, housework (vigorous vacuuming we might say), walking the children to school, all of these will ensure we keep sufficiently on the move.

Let us take a moment to examine the health benefits of even that minimum amount of exercise. Our chances of developing type 2 diabetes are cut in half and cut the chances of heart disease or suffering a stroke by over a third. We are more likely to live longer and some studies indicate we may reduce our chances of getting cancer by up to a half. Our bones and muscles will serve us better and for longer.

Mentally, we cut our risk of depression and of getting dementia by a third.

These benefits are all IN ADDITION TO the benefits we are already receiving from intermittent fasting (see the discussions in earlier chapters).

It is an often said, yet an extremely accurate truism, that

our lives are increasingly sedentary. One of the best ways to get exercise is to fit it into our everyday lives. Walk instead of drive; do some strength building exercises when we get up in the morning. If we drive to work, park the car at the end of the parking lot rather than by the entrance to your office. Stroll out to a shop to get lunch or fit in a walk during your lunch break. Exercise releases endorphins and fresh air awaken the brain. We find our afternoon performance is much improved if we have exercised during the middle of the day.

But exercise and intermittent fasting are not just two things we can do that are good for us. Most modern thinking agrees that there is a link between fasting and exercise which provides additional benefits for all the things we seek to achieve with the two activities. The sum of combining the two is greater than the individual benefits they each offer. That is synergy. With fasting and exercise combined, 2 + 2 equals 5!

We burn more calories, see better internal cell repair, and see greater mental health benefits.

This is because modern thinking is challenging the age-old belief that we should not exercise on an empty stomach. When our parents told us as children not to swim after eating lunch, they were speaking more sense than they intended. Exercise-wise, a swim before lunch would have offered much better results (not that we probably needed to worry as children). What the latest research is showing is that it is actually better to exercise on an empty stomach.

To conclude this section: if we exercise during our fast, the total benefit is greater than the sum of its separate parts.

Intermittent Fasting 16/8

Best exercise to enhance the advantages of fasting

To get a little (but not too) scientific for a moment, the speed at which we burn fat is determined by our sympathetic nervous system (SNS). Two things stimulate our SNS: one is the exercise itself, the other is not having a stomach full of food. Thus, when we fast and exercise, we are initiating a combination of fat burning pressures. But there are more. Oxidative stress increases, which promotes muscle growth and strength. Leaner. Better. Stronger.

We can fine-tune this even more if we plan our exercise routines carefully.

Fasting Days: These should be used to undertake your low-intensity exercise. There are two reasons for this: 1) If your sugar levels have fallen, then dizziness can strike with too much exercise. 2) If the body is desperately looking for something to burn to create energy, it may attack muscle mass, which is something we want to keep. Therefore, fasting days are great for doing walks, light swimming, and gentle jogs.

Non-Fasting Days: It is therefore logical that we save our high-intensity workouts for days when we have eaten. These are the times to hit the gym, to go for that long run, or to rip through our laps in the pool.

Weights: If weights form part of our exercise regime, then do this on our non-fasting days. Similarly, if we are looking for high-intensity short burst exercise, such as circuit training, non-fast days should be used. Also, with these types of workouts, we should ideally eat within thirty minutes after our exercise.

The joy of intermittent fasting for many people is that it is easy and flexible. For those on a serious weight loss or muscle building program, the advice above is necessary to achieve the results we seek. But for most of us looking to get fitter, healthier, and a little lighter on our feet, it is enough to remember that any exercise is good for us, no matter what form it takes.

Chapter 10: Intermittent Fasting and the Ketogenic Diet

Why is eating fat so good for losing weight? Fats, carbs, and proteins are known as the "macronutrients" and they affect our bodies in different ways. Fat by far is the most filling and calorie-rich food and helps us consume overall less daily by inhibiting the eating of other types of food. In fact, scientifically, one gram of protein or carbohydrates provides four calories, while one gram of fat provides nine calories.

A ketogenic diet is a high-fat, low-carb method of eating. (It is similar to the Atkins and low-carb diet, but critically different in this way.) Basically, by drastically reducing your body's intake of carbohydrates and replacing them with fat, you are putting your body in a state known as "ketosis." Although there are several variations of this diet, normally it consists of eating 75% fat, 20% protein, and only 5% carbohydrates. I will call these proportions the "standard" ketogenic diet.

There are three other types of well-known ketogenic diets:

1.   The cyclical ketogenic diet involves having five ketogenic days followed by two high-carb days.

2.   The targeted ketogenic diet (to be described here) is an adaptation that allows you to add carbs around your workouts.

3.   Finally, the high-protein ketogenic diet is similar to the standard ketogenic diet but includes a lot more

protein. For this one, the proportions of the major components are 60% fat, 35% protein, and 5% carbs.

The ketogenic diet and the advent of intermittent fasting were first written about in ancient Greek and Indian medical texts. Hippocrates' famous quote, "Let food be thy medicine, and medicine be thy food" was an early indication of the recognition of the importance of diet and nutrition on human overall health. The first study on ketogenic diets was done in France in 1911 on epileptics. At that time, epileptic patients were customarily given dangerous doses of potassium bromide, which resulted in major toxicity in the brain. They took 20 patients and gave them a low carbohydrate, vegan diet and found that although only a few patients reduced their seizures, the majority of them had improved mental abilities. With the rise of allopathic medicine leading to the discovery of anticonvulsant drugs, these nutritional therapies were abandoned. But after seeing 20-30% of adult patients who were epileptic since childhood still with seizures in spite of the medication, the ketogenic diet was reintroduced, again with success. There is now no question the benefit of a ketogenic diet for childhood epileptic syndromes (such as West, Lennox-Gastaut, and Dravet) has been 30-40% effective based on current medical statistics.

Ketogenic diets have also been shown to help with Parkinson's disease, Alzheimer's disease, and dementia. Currently, researchers are looking at "ketone bodies" in the human blood and their health benefits. What they have found is beta-hydroxybutyrate (BHB), the most prominent ketone body, has the capacity to cross the blood-brain barrier and to be used for fuel for the brain similar to glucose or sugar. In fact, research has shown BHB to be more efficient (producing more energy per gram) than glucose. One medical doctor, Mary Newport, made the claim that she has reversed her husband's Alzheimer's disease using coconut oil. One of the main components of a ketogenic diet is consuming large amounts of fat, the most recommended fat being coconut oil. Large research studies are underway at major universities on the effects of coconut oil and mild chain triglycerides (a component of coconut oil) on cognitive function and impairment disorders. The results have been very promising.

What does this mean for intermittent fasting, ketogenic diets, weight loss, and performance? It means that if you follow these protocols, not only do you improve your physical health, but also your mental and emotional health. Hundreds and thousands of people have found relief and healing from many horrible illnesses and conditions by changing what, why, how, and at what frequency they eat.

In general, a ketogenic diet prescribes users to:

• Avoid these foods: potatoes, rice, breads, pastas, cereals, grains, tortillas (flour or corn), fruit and fruit juices, soy products, fried foods, processed foods, refined sugars ("sodas"), chips and cookies, crackers and dips, alcohol, artificial ingredients, and artificial sweeteners. I know this sounds like a lot, but stay with me.

• Stick to these foods: Meats, fish, eggs, butter, nuts and seeds, coconut and avocados, cheese, heavy and sour cream, chicken and beef bone broths, low-carb veggies such as cauliflower, celery, onion, cabbage, bell peppers, squash, spinach, zucchini, and water, coffee or tea. Try to stick to organic, grass-fed, and cage-free products, if possible. It is best to stick to whole, single-ingredient foods for your meals. For instance, dark chocolate (~70% cacao) is a good treatment for people seeking to go into ketosis. Use these lists as a guide. There is "a ton" of information on ketogenic diets out there on the internet, including many excellent ketogenic recipes.

Similarly to intermittent fasting, a ketogenic diet has been shown to increase insulin sensitivity in the cells of the body, which lowers blood sugar. An advantage over traditional diets is its emphasis on the assimilation of fats of various types. Since intermittent fasting and the ketogenic diet have similar impacts on your body (getting it to use stored fat as energy instead of the food you just consumed) it only makes sense to try combining them.

If you are interested in trying intermittent fasting while using the ketogenic diet, keep the following things in mind:

• Do not start both of them at the same time. Learn from the mistakes of others and from mine. Your body needs to get adapted to the ketogenic diet before it is required to go through long periods of time without eating. I recommend at first taking two weeks to get accustomed to the ketogenic diet without doing any purposeful fasting, and subsequently combine it with an intermittent fasting schedule best suited for you.

• Start out slow and go with what feels natural. You might automatically begin to detoxify or cleanse out in what is called a "Herxheimer reaction." Once your body adjusts to using up fat reserves and becomes "fat-adapted" you will start to feel less hungry. Try starting out by not snacking between meals before moving on to skipping a whole meal.

• Keep yourself busy. Do not spend a lot of time hanging in and around your kitchen or supermarkets, and plan plenty of things to do to keep yourself busy. Do not surround yourself with temptation and get "out of the house" as often as you can.

• Cook and prepare several of your meals in advance. It's always easier to sit down and eat when you have prepared efficiently. Food preparation is much easier if you eat the same things three to four times a week. Getting a crock-pot was one of the best investments I ever made. Without much time involved, it helps me to cook lots of food, and I store it for later. One of my favorite cookware inventions of late is the Instapot. (Click here to order.)

• Do not expect your new diet and intermittent fasting to fix everything you might be ailing from. It definitely will help you lose weight and to be healthier. But, simultaneously, you should also be working on your stress levels and on getting enough sleep (you know when you need more sleep and it varies from person to person). And it's best if you can include purposeful exercise in your weekly schedule.

Chapter 11: Extra Tips to Get the Most Out of Intermittent Fasting

Congratulations on reaching this part of the book! If you have followed through up until this point, then you should know by now just how beneficial intermittent fasting can be. You might have already started to implement the strategies and recipes that I have shared with you. If so, then good for you. You are on your way to a better and healthier life, a lower body weight, a better body composition, and let's not forget a reduced risk of many diseases.

Before we finish off however, I do have a few final tips that I would like to share with you. The information I have provided here is already invaluable because it will put you on the right path to lose weight successfully through both diet and the intermittent fasting program. But what I am about to share with you will ultimately help to speed up your results and give you an even greater goal to look forward to.

Adjust your diet plan as you go

I shared an excellent diet plan with you in this book, and it is perfectly normal and okay to follow the plan for the full two weeks that I have designed it for. Even after that, you may continue with the program in order to experience more benefits, such as reduced body weight and to gain an improvement in your overall health.

Intermittent Fasting 16/8

Now, at the same time, I do want to note that following one single plan over an extended period of time will often not offer you the best results that you could achieve through intermittent fasting.

The thing is every person is different; you are unique. For this reason, a specific meal plan that works for you will likely not be ideal for every single person.

This means that the diet program that I introduce in this book might be able to work, but you may need to make some modifications as you go along in order to achieve the specific goals that you have in mind with the program that you are implementing.

Sure, you are not a dietician with years of experience in the industry, which really does make it somewhat harder for you to develop an appropriate diet plan that will suit you and help you achieve the goals you are striving toward. This, however, does not necessarily mean that it will be impossible for you to make simple adjustments in order to reach those weight loss goals.

Here's an example: you follow the diet plan that I have offered here and prepare the specific meals that I have provided you with. Even though you implement these meal plans every day and you avoid binge eating, you find that you are not losing a lot of weight. In this case, there might not be an appropriate caloric deficit in your weight management plan.

When a caloric deficit is not present, it means you won't be able to lose weight—we have covered this already in a previous chapter in the book. If this is the case with you, then it means you will need to adjust your diet to reduce your daily caloric intake. This will essentially improve your caloric deficit and ensure you can lose weight more effectively through your intermittent fasting weight loss plan.

Don't overlook the importance of exercise in a weight loss strategy

I have seen a lot of people start with an intermittent fasting plan and end up complaining that the program is not working for them. The same person would then tell me that they do not have a very physical lifestyle.

You should have already read the topic where I explained how intermittent fasting is used for weight loss, so you should understand that without expending calories each day, you won't be able to lose that excess fat that has accumulated inside your body.

Expending calories mean being physically active. Unfortunately, quite a large percentage of the worldwide population are living sedentary lifestyles. With a sedentary lifestyle, you are really "paving the way" for weight gain. If you are not physically active, you won't be able to burn an adequate number of calories each day for weight loss to be possible in the first place.

Thus, when you decide to follow my intermittent fasting weight loss cookbook and meal plan, then you should be sure to also include an appropriate exercise plan. Make sure you are physically active according to the prescribed standards. At a minimum, you should be physically active on a few days each week.

The more you exercise, the more calories you will burn, of course. At the same time, you should be sure not to overdo things in terms of physical activity. There really is no use in causing yourself injury due to overtraining, this will only lead to temporary disability and will make training harder for the next few days (sometimes weeks or months, if you suffer a more serious injury).

It is best to create a balanced exercise plan for yourself and then test it out. Listen to your body and understand when you are pushing yourself too hard, as well as when you have some extra capacity available to up your game at the gym.

You will have to take your daily calorie consumption into account here (we discussed how you can calculate your ideal daily calorie requirement in a previous section). This data will definitely come in handy. Calculate an appropriate exercise plan that will ensure that your daily caloric expenditure through physical exercise will reach past your daily caloric intake.

Deal with hunger pangs like a boss

Let's tackle a topic that you will likely face. Hunger pangs are something that we all experience when we first start out with an intermittent fasting plan. You suddenly have to get your body adjusted to an entirely new way of eating. No longer do you get up in the morning and cook some eggs and bacon. You have to get up and drink water, or perhaps have a cup of coffee, but you'll have to wait until the afternoon before you get to have your first meal.

So the question now is, should you give in to the temptation that you will be experiencing, especially during those first few days? Or should you implement an appropriate strategy to help you better cope with these hunger pangs and the cravings that you are going to experience?

There are different strategies that you can use to cope with your cravings. One would be to drink a glass of water if you feel hungry and you feel those cravings building up. This is an effective strategy for lots of people, but not for everyone, of course. If you find that plain water or even filtered water does not work well for you, then I suggest you try some carbonated water. Be sure not to opt for carbonated water with added sweetening agents, as these are loaded with carbs. Rather, just opt for plain sparkling water. The carbonation in the water can help to make you feel full for a while to ensure you can make it to your eating window without giving in to your temptations.

It is important that you are patient and practice self-control when cravings start building up. Giving in to these cravings should not be considered okay now-and-then, as this will break the fasting window and it will yield less effective results compared to ensuring you last until you are inside of your feeding window.

Avoid eating these foods

With intermittent fasting, a lot of people tend to follow their usual eating habits in terms of the specific foods that they put on their plate during each meal, expecting that they will lose weight just because they have fasted during the morning, night, and a part of the afternoon.

While intermittent fasting may help to improve metabolism and support digestive function that will ultimately improve your ability to lose weight, the food you eat still counts. As you might have noted, the meal plans that I shared with you in this book generally combine a range of healthy foods in order to ensure you get the nutrients you need without loading up on too many carbs. I did include a lot of delicious options that you can try out.

Just as there are a lot of foods that you can surely include in your diet to help you lose that extra weight that is causing you concern, there are also some foods that you should always try to avoid if your goal is to lose weight.

Below, I would like to share some of the most important foods that you should try to exclude from your diet in order to improve the results you are able to achieve when you implement the recipes and meal plans I have provided.

• Fried foods, of course, are at the top of my list. There is no doubt that fried foods are one particularly common reason why the world is so obese. Millions of people eat fried foods as much as every day. This does not only cause them to gain weight, but also to experience a rise in cholesterol levels, be at a higher risk of heart disease, and more.

• Fast foods, along with fried foods, since most chains that offer fast foods tend to deep-fry their food in the worst types of oil and fat to make them more "tasty" for the general public. Unfortunately, this also adds more fat to your belly, thighs, arms, and other areas of your body.

• Corn is another food that really isn't the best choice for people who are trying to lose weight. Sure, it is not an unhealthy food, but consider the fact that this is a type of grain that is relatively high in sugar. The sugar spike experienced when you eat corn leads to the release of insulin, triggering inflammation and taking you one step closer to the dreadful complications of insulin resistance.

In addition to all of these, be sure to be wary of added sugars in everything you eat. For example, if you visit your local supermarket and grab a health bar to use as the food to break your fast, the fact that the word "healthy" appears on the bar does not necessarily mean it is truly healthy.

Always look at the ingredients of what you buy and what you will be putting into your body. Making your own healthy energy bars at home might be a better solution as well.

30-day Intermittent Fasting Meal Plan

The 16:8 intermittent fasting method is the most popular choice because it tends to be the easiest one to follow. Since it is the most popular, and it will more than likely be the one that you choose to follow, I am going to provide you with a 30-day schedule for the 16:8 protocol to help you get started with you intermittent fasting diet.

I will put times in this schedule, but you can easily change them to suit your personal needs. The point is that you will reduce your eating window to an eight-hour period. You are also allowed to eat whatever foods and beverages you like during that eight-hour window and as many meals as you want. The schedule below will provide you with a sample menu to help you out with some healthier options, though.

You don't have to restrict your calorie intake either, but it is recommended that you:

•   Eat a certain combination of different foods that provide you with lots of nutrients, such as vegetables and fruits, high-fiber whole grains, lean protein, and healthy fats.

•   Consume at least the recommended amount of water during the day. This includes the hours where you don't get to eat as well. Water is a freebie in every diet.

This challenge will also give you an eight-minute exercise routine that you can do before your first meal of the day to help boost the effects of the fast. This workout is comprised of cardio and resistance training intervals. Without further ado, here is your 30-Day 16:8 intermittent fasting protocol.

Day 1

- Wake Up – Coffee, green tea, or zero calorie detox drink.
- Breakfast 1:00 p.m. – Scrambled eggs with toast.
- Snack 2:30 p.m. – One serving of almonds and an orange.
- Dinner 8:00 p.m. – Grilled chicken and veggies, and bread pudding for dessert.

Day 2

- Wake Up – Coffee, green tea, or zero calorie detox drink.
- Breakfast 1:00 p.m. – Avocado toast with tomato, bacon, and egg.
- Snack 2:30 p.m. – Cucumber and watermelon salad.
- Dinner 8:00 p.m. – Baked fish and veggies, and ice cream for dessert.

Day 3

- Wake Up – Coffee, green tea, or zero calorie detox drink.
- Breakfast 1:00 p.m. – Kale, banana, and peanut butter smoothie.

- o Snack 2:30 p.m. – Medium-sized dark chocolate brownie.
- o Dinner 8:00 p.m. – Asian-style chicken soup and fruit custard for dessert.

Day 4

- o Wake Up – Coffee, green tea, or zero calorie detox drink.
- o Breakfast 1:00 p.m. – Breakfast sandwich on whole-wheat toast.
- o Snack 2:30 p.m. – Serving of mixed nuts.
- o Dinner 8:00 p.m. – Kidney bean chili with two to three chapattis, and a dark chocolate brownie for dessert.

Day 5

- o Wake Up – Coffee, green tea, or zero calorie detox drink.
- o Breakfast 1:00 p.m. – Tofu scramble with tomato.
- o Snack 2:30 p.m. – Four almonds and an apple.
- o Dinner 8:00 p.m. – Grilled chicken and veggies, and ice cream for dessert.

Day 6

- o Wake Up – Coffee, green tea, or zero calorie detox drink.
- o Breakfast 1:00 p.m. – Scrambled eggs with peanut butter toast.

- o Snack 2:30 p.m. – Small bowl of nachos with a low-fat dip.
- o Dinner 8:00 p.m. – Vegetable lasagna with bread pudding for dessert.

Day 7

- o Wake Up – Coffee, green tea, or zero calorie detox drink.
- o Breakfast 1:00 p.m. – Bacon and eggs with whole-wheat toast.
- o Snack 2:30 p.m. – One serving of almonds and an orange.
- o Dinner 8:00 p.m. – Tuna sandwich with a low-fat milkshake for dessert.

Day 8

- o Wake Up – Coffee, green tea, or zero calorie detox drink.
- o Breakfast 1:00 p.m. – Wheat flakes and milk.
- o Snack 2:30 p.m. – One serving of mixed nuts.
- o Dinner 8:00 p.m. – Grilled chicken tortilla wrap and bread pudding for dessert.

Day 9

- o Wake Up – Coffee, green tea, or zero calorie detox drink.
- o Breakfast 1:00 p.m. – Kale, strawberry, and blueberry smoothie.

- o   Snack 2:30 p.m. – Cucumber and watermelon salad.
- o   Dinner 8:00 p.m. – Kidney bean chili and fruit custard for dessert.

Day 10

- o   Wake Up – Coffee, green tea, or zero calorie detox drink.
- o   Breakfast 1:00 p.m. – Scrambled eggs with toast.
- o   Snack 2:30 p.m. – A medium-sized dark chocolate brownie
- o   Dinner 8:00 p.m. – Baked fish and veggies with low-fat frozen yogurt for dessert.

Day 11

- o   Wake Up – Coffee, green tea, or zero calorie detox drink.
- o   Breakfast 1:00 p.m. – Avocado toast with sliced chicken breast and tomato.
- o   Snack 2:30 p.m. – Apple and watermelon.
- o   Dinner 8:00 p.m. – Grilled chicken and veggie kebab with ice cream for dessert.

Day 12

- o   Wake Up – Coffee, green tea, or zero calorie detox drink.
- o   Breakfast 1:00 p.m. – Breakfast sandwich on whole-wheat toast.

- Snack 2:30 p.m. – A small bowl of nachos with a low-fat dip.
- Dinner 8:00 p.m. – Buffalo chicken tortilla wrap with a fresh fruit salad for dessert.

Day 13

- Wake Up – Coffee, green tea, or zero calorie detox drink.
- Breakfast 1:00 p.m. – Scrambled eggs with peanut butter toast.
- Snack 2:30 p.m. – A small bowl of potato wafers.
- Dinner 8:00 p.m. – Indian lentil soup with fruit custard for dessert.

Day 14

- Wake Up – Coffee, green tea, or zero calorie detox drink.
- Breakfast 1:00 p.m. – Curried tofu scramble.
- Snack 2:30 p.m. – Four almonds and an apple.
- Dinner 8:00 p.m. – Baked chicken with roasted vegetables and a side salad with a dark chocolate brownie for dessert.

Day 15

- Wake Up – Coffee, green tea, or zero calorie detox drink.

- o Breakfast 1:00 p.m. – Bacon, egg, avocado, and whole-wheat toast.
- o Snack 2:30 p.m. – Cucumber and watermelon salad.
- o Dinner 8:00 p.m. – Vegetable lasagna with a low-fat milkshake for dessert.

Day 16

- o Wake Up – Coffee, green tea, or zero calorie detox drink.
- o Breakfast 1:00 p.m. – Scrambled eggs with toast.
- o Snack 2:30 p.m. – Four almonds and an orange.
- o Dinner 8:00 p.m. – Grilled chicken and veggies, and bread pudding for dessert.

Day 17

- o Wake Up – Coffee, green tea, or zero calorie detox drink.
- o Breakfast 1:00 p.m. – Avocado toast with tomato, bacon, and egg.
- o Snack 2:30 p.m. – Cucumber and watermelon salad.
- o Dinner 8:00 p.m. – Baked fish and veggies, and ice cream for dessert.

Day 18

- o Wake Up – Coffee, green tea, or zero calorie detox drink.

- Breakfast 1:00 p.m. – Kale, banana, and peanut butter smoothie.
- Snack 2:30 p.m. – Medium-sized dark chocolate brownie.
- Dinner 8:00 p.m. – Asian-style chicken soup and fruit custard for dessert.

Day 19

- Wake Up – Coffee, green tea, or zero calorie detox drink.
- Breakfast 1:00 p.m. – Breakfast sandwich on whole-wheat toast.
- Snack 2:30 p.m. – Small bowl of popcorn.
- Dinner 8:00 p.m. – Kidney bean chili with two to three chapattis, and a dark chocolate brownie for dessert.

Day 20

- Wake Up – Coffee, green tea, or zero calorie detox drink.
- Breakfast 1:00 p.m. – Tofu scramble with tomato.
- Snack 2:30 p.m. – Four almonds and an apple.
- Dinner 8:00 p.m. – Grilled chicken and veggies and ice cream for dessert.

Day 21

- Wake Up – Coffee, green tea, or zero calorie detox drink.

- o Breakfast 1:00 p.m. – Scrambled eggs with peanut butter toast.
- o Snack 2:30 p.m. – Small bowl of nachos with a low-fat dip.
- o Dinner 8:00 p.m. – Vegetable lasagna with bread pudding for dessert.

Day 22

- o Wake Up – Coffee, green tea, or zero calorie detox drink.
- o Breakfast 1:00 p.m. – Bacon and eggs with whole-wheat toast.
- o Snack 2:30 p.m. – Four almonds and an orange.
- o Dinner 8:00 p.m. – Tuna sandwich with a low-fat milkshake for dessert.

Day 23

- o Wake Up – Coffee, green tea, or zero calorie detox drink.
- o Breakfast 1:00 p.m. – Wheat flakes and milk.
- o Snack 2:30 p.m. – Small bowl of popcorn.
- o Dinner 8:00 p.m. – Grilled chicken tortilla wrap and bread pudding for dessert.

Day 24

- o Wake Up – Coffee, green tea, or zero calorie detox drink.
- o Breakfast 1:00 p.m. – Kale, strawberry, and blueberry smoothie.

- o Snack 2:30 p.m. – Cucumber and watermelon salad.
- o Dinner 8:00 p.m. – Kidney bean chili and fruit custard for dessert.

Day 25

- o Wake Up – Coffee, green tea, or zero calorie detox drink.
- o Breakfast 1:00 p.m. – Scrambled eggs with toast.
- o Snack 2:30 p.m. – A medium-sized dark chocolate brownie
- o Dinner 8:00 p.m. – Baked fish and veggies with low-fat frozen yogurt for dessert.

Day 26

- o Wake Up – Coffee, green tea, or zero calorie detox drink.
- o Breakfast 1:00 p.m. – Avocado toast with sliced chicken breast and tomato.
- o Snack 2:30 p.m. – Apple and watermelon.
- o Dinner 8:00 p.m. – Grilled chicken and veggie kebab with ice cream for dessert.

Day 27

- o Wake Up – Coffee, green tea, or zero calorie detox drink.
- o Breakfast 1:00 p.m. – Breakfast sandwich on whole-wheat toast.

o   Snack 2:30 p.m. – A small bowl of nachos with a low-fat dip.
o   Dinner 8:00 p.m. – Buffalo chicken tortilla wrap with a fresh fruit salad for dessert.

Day 28

o   Wake Up – Coffee, green tea, or zero calorie detox drink.
o   Breakfast 1:00 p.m. – Scrambled eggs with peanut butter toast.
o   Snack 2:30 p.m. – A small bowl of potato wafers.
o   Dinner 8:00 p.m. – Indian lentil soup with fruit custard for dessert.

Day 29

o   Wake Up – Coffee, green tea, or zero calorie detox drink.
o   Breakfast 1:00 p.m. – Curried tofu scramble.
o   Snack 2:30 p.m. – Four almonds and an apple.
o   Dinner 8:00 p.m. – Baked chicken with roasted vegetables and a side salad with a dark chocolate brownie for dessert.

Day 30

o   Wake Up – Coffee, green tea, or zero calorie detox drink.

Intermittent Fasting 16/8

o Breakfast 1:00 p.m. – Bacon, egg, avocado, and whole-wheat toast.
o Snack 2:30 p.m. – Cucumber and watermelon salad.
o Dinner 8:00 p.m. – Vegetable lasagna with a low-fat milkshake for dessert.

Intermittent Fasting Recipes

Breakfast Broccoli Muffins

Ingredients:

- 2 teaspoons ghee, soft

- 2 eggs

- 2 cups almond flour

- 1 cup broccoli florets, chopped

- 1 cup almond milk

- 2 tablespoons nutritional yeast

- 1 teaspoon baking powder

Directions:

1. In a bowl, mix the eggs with the flour, broccoli, milk, yeast, and baking powder and stir really well.

2. Grease a muffin tray with the ghee, divide broccoli mix, introduce in the oven and cook at 350 degrees F for 30 minutes.

3. Serve these muffins for breakfast.

Breakfast Pork Bagel

Ingredients:

- 1 yellow onion, chopped

- 1 tablespoon ghee

- 2 pounds pork meat, ground

- 2 eggs

- $^2/_3$ cup tomato sauce

- a pinch of salt and black pepper

- 1 teaspoon sweet paprika

Directions:

1.   Heat up a pan with the ghee over medium heat, add onion, stir, and cook for 3-4 minutes.

2.   In a bowl, combine the meat with sautéed onions, eggs, tomato sauce, salt, pepper, and paprika, stir well and shape 6 bagels using your hands.

3.   Arrange the meat bagels on a lined baking sheet and cook them in the oven at 400 degrees F for 40 minutes.

4.   Divide the bagels between plates and serve them for breakfast.

Intermittent Fasting 16/8

Easy Baked Eggs

Ingredients:

- 1 cup baby spinach

- 4 ounces bacon, chopped

- 8 eggs, whisked

- a pinch of salt and black pepper

Directions:

1.   Heat up a pan over medium-high heat, add bacon, stir, and brown it for 4 minutes.

2.   Add baby spinach, salt, and pepper, toss, cook for 1 minute more, take off the heat and divide into 4 ramekins.

3.   Divide whisked eggs in each ramekin, introduce them all in the oven and cook at 400 degrees F for 15 minutes.

4.   Serve the baked eggs for breakfast.

Eggs and Meat Patties

Ingredients:

- ¾ pound pork, ground

- ¼ pound beef liver, ground

- ½ pound beef, ground

- 1 tablespoon maple syrup

- ½ teaspoon sage, dried

- ½ teaspoon rosemary, dried

- ½ teaspoon thyme, dried

- a pinch of salt and black pepper

- 4 eggs

- 2 tablespoons olive oil

Directions:

1.   In a bowl, combine the pork with the beef, beef liver, maple syrup, sage, rosemary, thyme, salt and pepper, stir and shape 4 patties out of this mix.

2.   Heat up a pan with half of the oil over medium-high heat, add meat patties, cook them for 5 minutes on each side and divide them between plates.

3.   Heat up the same pan with the rest of the oil, crack the eggs, fry them, divide them next to the patties, and serve for breakfast.

Cauliflower Cakes

Ingredients:

*   1 cauliflower head, florets separated

* $2/3$ cup almond flour

*   1 tablespoon nutritional yeast

*   2 eggs

*   ½ teaspoon turmeric powder

*   2 tablespoons ghee

*   a pinch of salt and black pepper

Directions:

1.   Put the cauliflower florets in a pot, add water to cover them, bring to a boil over medium heat, cook for 8 minutes, drain well, put the cauliflower in your food processor and pulse well.

2.   In a bowl, combine the cauliflower with the flour, eggs, yeast, salt, pepper, and turmeric powder, stir well and shape medium patties out of this mix.

3.   Heat up a pan with the ghee over medium-high heat, add the patties, cook them for 3 minutes on each side, divide them between plates, and serve for breakfast.

Beef, Avocado, and Eggs

Ingredients:

*   8 mushrooms, sliced

*   1 yellow onion, chopped

*   1 tablespoon olive oil

*   3 ounces beef, ground

*   a pinch of salt and black pepper

*   2 eggs, whisked

*   ½ teaspoon smoked paprika

*   1 avocado, peeled, pitted, and chopped

*   10 black olives, pitted and sliced

Directions:

1.   Heat up a pan with the oil over medium-high heat, add beef, stir and brown for 4-5 minutes.

2.   Add mushrooms and onion, stir, and cook for 3 minutes more.

3.   Add salt, pepper, paprika, and the eggs; toss, cook for 3-4 minutes more, divide into bowls, top each bowl with avocado and olives, and serve for breakfast.

A Large Coleslaw with a Homemade, Very Low-Carb Dressing

Ingredients:

- 1 cup mayonnaise (read labels and choose a low carb option)

- 1 cup sour cream (low carb option)

- 3 tablespoons of apple cider vinegar

- stevia or sweetener to taste

- salt and pepper to taste

Directions:

1. Add mayonnaise, sour cream, and apple cider vinegar to a bowl.

2. Blend well.

3. Add sweetener or stevia. Add pepper and salt to taste

Keto 90-Second Sandwich Bread

Ingredients:

- 1 tablespoon butter

- 3 tablespoons almond flour

- 1 teaspoon psyllium powder

- 1 egg

- a small dash of salt

Directions:

1.   In the microwave melt the butter for 20 seconds (in the small baking dish).

2.   Add the psyllium powder, almond flour, baking powder, salt, and egg to the baking dish.

3.   Mix the ingredients thoroughly with a fork.

4.   Place in the dish in the microwave on high for 90 seconds.

5.   Remove the bread from the dish and slice down the middle to form your two sandwich pieces.

6.   Consider crisping the bread up in a hot skillet with butter if you are taking your sandwich in more of a grilled direction.

Keto Cheese Popcorn: Low-Carb Cheese Pops

You can choose the cheese of your choice. Hard cheese will dry out a little faster.

Directions:

1.   Cube cheese into uniform cubes, about the size of the end of your pinky.

2.   Spread cubes out on a sheet to dry.

3.   Allow the cheese cubes to dehydrate thoroughly on a shelf, usually 3-4 days.

4.   Preheat the oven to 400 degrees F.

5.   Bake your cheese and listen to those pops! You'll start hearing them in 2 minutes or so. Bake for about 30 minutes.

Butter Coffee

Ingredients:

*   1 cup of water

*   2 tablespoons coffee

*   1 tablespoon grass-fed butter

*   1 tablespoon coconut oil

Directions:

1.   Make a cup of coffee in your favorite way. A Turkish coffee cup is preferable. Simmer ground coffee in water for about five minutes and then strain it into a cup. You can also use a Moka pot, a French press, or a coffee machine.

2.   Pour your brewed coffee into your blender (like a NutriBullet) with butter and coconut oil. Blend for about ten seconds. You would see it instantly become light and creamy.

3.   Pour the butter coffee into a mug and enjoy! Add any ingredient of your choice like cinnamon or whipped cream.

Avocado Toast

Ingredients:

- low-carb bread (makes 12 slices)

- ½ tablespoon unsalted butter (melted)

- 2 tablespoons of coconut oil

- 7 large eggs

- 1 tablespoon of baking powder

- 2 cups of almond flour

- ½ tablespoon of xanthan gum

- ½ tablespoon of sea salt

- 1 medium avocado

- avocado rose and topping

- 2 tablespoons of sunflower seeds

- sea salt

Directions for low-carb bread:

1.   Preheat your oven to 350 degrees F. Beat the egg for 1 to 2 minutes with an electric mixer on high speed.

2.   Add coconut oil and melted butter (let it cool a bit so that you don't cook the eggs).

3.   Add the remaining bread ingredients. Note: the

batter will become quite thick.

4.   Pour the batter into a loaf pan lined with parchment paper.

5.   Bake for 45 minutes or until a skewer comes out of the middle clean.

Avocado Rose and Topping

•   Once you are ready to make the rest of the recipe, set two slices of the low-carb bread to toast to your desired crispiness.

•   Cut an avocado in half lengthwise and remove the pit. Peel the avocado shell away carefully.

•   Laying the avocado halves flat side down, begin slicing it thinly until the whole avocado is sliced.

•   Working with one avocado half at a time, gently push the slices, fanning them out into long strips of overlapping slices.

•   Then, roll the strip into a spiral until the whole thing comes into the shape of a round rose.

•   Top each slice of toast with an avocado rose and a sprinkle of sea salt and sunflower seeds. Enjoy one toast and avocado rose per person.

Pumpkin Spice Walnut Bread

Ingredients:

- 2 cups of almond flour

- ½ cup coconut flour

- ½ cup erythritol

- 1 tablespoon baking powder

- 1 ½ teaspoons pumpkin pie spice

- 1 pinch sea salt

- 1 cup pumpkin puree

- ¾ cup melted butter

- $^1/_3$ cup heavy cream

- 4 large eggs

- ¼ cup chopped walnuts

Directions:

- Preheat the oven to 350 degrees F and grease a loaf pan. Combine the coconut flour, almond flour, sugar-free sweetener, pumpkin pie spice, baking powder, and salt, and whisk well in a bowl.

- In a food processor, combine the pumpkin butter, heavy cream, and eggs, then blend smooth.

- Whisk the wet ingredients into the dry mix, then

fold into walnuts.

•   Pour the batter into the pan and bake for 55 to 65 minutes until a knife inserted in the center comes out clean.

•   Turn off the oven and let the loaf cool for 15 minutes.

•   Remove the loaf and turn it out into a wire rack to cool completely. Then cut into 12 slices.

Lemon Poppy Seed Pancake

Ingredients:

Pancakes

- 13 oz. whole milk ricotta cheese

- 6 large eggs

- 2 large lemons (zested and juiced)

- 1 ½ teaspoons vanilla extract

- 25 drops liquid stevia

- 1 ½ teaspoons baking powder

- ½ cup almond flour

- 1 ½ tablespoons poppy seeds

- ¼ teaspoon sea salt

Lemon glaze

- ½ cup powdered erythritol

- ½ lemon (juiced)

- 1 splash almond milk

Directions:

- Zest an entire lemon and squeeze the juice out. Reserve half for the lemon glaze.

- In a food processor, combine all the wet

ingredients, plus half the lemon juice and all of the zest, and blend for a few seconds or blend until well-mixed.

• Heat up a large griddle to medium heat and using a quarter cup measuring cup to portion the batter.

.

Main Meals

Slow Cooker Chili with Cauliflower Rice

Ingredients:

• 1 pound 80% lean ground beef

• 1 pound ground sausage

• 2 small green peppers (diced)

• 1 small yellow onion

• 2 cups diced tomatoes

• 2 tablespoons chili powder

• 1 teaspoon ground cumin

• ¼ cup of water

• salt and pepper

• 1 large head cauliflower

• 1 tablespoon olive oil

• green onion (optional)

• fresh chilies (optional)

Directions:

• Cook the sausage and beef in a skillet, then drain the fat when it turns brown.

•   Spread the mixture in the bottom of a slow cooker.

•   Add the peppers, onion, tomatoes, chili powder, cumin, and water.

•   Season liberally with salt and water, then stir well and cover. Cook on low heat for 6-8 hours.

•   Place the cauliflower in a food processor and pulse into rice-like grains.

•   Sauté the cauliflower in olive oil until tender (about 5-8 minutes) then serve alongside the chili garnish with green onion and fresh chilies if you like.

Roasted Pork Belly Bites with Braised Cabbage

Ingredients:

- 2 pounds pork belly

- 2 teaspoons fennel seed

- 2 tablespoons olive oil

- salt

Braised cabbage:

- 2 tablespoon olive oil

- 2 cloves

- 1 star anise

- 2 teaspoons caraway seeds

- ¼ red cabbage

- ¼ white or savoy cabbage (finely shredded)

- 1 cup chicken stock

- 2 tablespoons red wine vinegar

Directions:

- Preheat oven to 425 degrees F.

- Using a very sharp knife, score the pork belly skin into 1-inch strips, taking care not to cut into the meat. Rub the pork belly all over with the oil, fennel seeds, salt, and pepper, taking care to rub the seasonings into the skin well.

• Place the pork belly onto a baking tray and cook for about 20 minutes or until the skin is just starting to crisp up.

• Reduce the heat to 325 degrees F and cook for a further 1 ½ - 2 hours until the pork is tender.

• Meanwhile, heat the oil in a large sauté pan over medium heat and add the olive oil, cloves, star anise, and caraway, and cook until popping gently.

• Then add the shredded cabbage and a large pinch of salt. Stir to coat and cook gently for about 5 minutes until the cabbage has softened slightly.

• Crank the heat back up to 425 degrees F and cook for a final 20 minutes until the skin is crispy and crackling. Remove from the oven and allow to rest for 10-15 minutes.

• Add the stock and simmer for about 10 minutes until the cabbage is cooked to your taste.

• Remove from the heat and drain any excess stock, then stir in the vinegar.

• Cut the pork belly into chunks and serve with the braised cabbage on the side.

Cheddar Chicken and Broccoli Casserole

Ingredients:

- 20 oz. chicken breast

- 2 tablespoon olive oil

- 2 cups broccoli (preferably frozen)

- ½ cup sour cream

- ½ cup heavy cream

- 1 cup cheddar cheese

- 1 oz. pork rinds

- salt

- pepper

- ½ teaspoon paprika

- 1 teaspoon oregano

Directions:

- Preheat your oven to 450 degrees F. If you are using fresh broccoli, set it to steam or boil for a few minutes to get it softer a bit faster. In this recipe, we will be using frozen broccoli and it turns out great without precooking.

- If you haven't shredded your chicken, simply cook your chicken breast in an oiled pan and use two forks to pull the chicken apart into more bite-sized pieces.

- Combine frozen broccoli florets, shredded chicken, sour cream, and olive oil in a deep mixing bowl. Mix to combine thoroughly.

- Place your chicken and broccoli in a greased 8 x 1 inch baking dish. Spread them into an even layer, pressing firmly.

- The casserole should be slightly packed. Drizzle the heavy cream over the entire layer. Add your seasoning of choice in this step as well. Salt, pepper, paprika, and oregano will work very well for this recipe.

- Add a cup of shredded cheddar cheese to the top of the casserole all the way up to the edges.

- In a ziplock bag, add 1 oz. of pork rinds and crush them with either your hands or a rolling pin. Add these crushed pork rinds over the shredded cheese for a crispy casserole top.

- Bake for about 20-25 minutes. The entire casserole should be bubbling slightly and the edges brown. Serve with a side of marinara sauce and enjoy.

Shepherd's Pie

Ingredients:

- ¼ cup oil

- 1 pound ground turkey

- lamb or beef

- ¼ cup yellow onion

- 3 cloves garlic (minced)

- ½ cup celery (chopped)

- 2 12 oz. packaged riced cauliflower (cooked and well-drained)

- 1 cup heavy cream

- 1 cup shredded cheese

- ¼ grated parmesan

- 1 teaspoon dried thyme

Directions:

- Warm the oil in a large skillet and in the warm pan, add the ground meat, onions, garlic, and celery. Sauté until the meat is fully browned.

- Turn off the heat and quickly stir in the tomatoes. Pour mixture to a casserole dish.

- Blend together the cheese, thyme, and cauliflower

in a food processor until you have a mixture that clearly resembles mashed potatoes instead of riced cauliflower.

•   Spread the cauliflower over the meat in the casserole dish.

•   Bake at 350 degrees F for 35-40 minutes.

•   Cool slightly, cut, and serve.

Almond Pesto Salmon

Ingredients:

- 1 tablespoon olive oil

- 1 clove garlic

- ¼ cup almonds

- ½ teaspoon parsley

- juice of half a lemon

- 2 6 oz. Atlantic salmon fillets

- 2 tablespoon butter

- ½ shallot

- 2 handfuls frisée

Directions:

- Start by making your almond pesto. In a food processor blend almonds, garlic, and pulse olive oil. Add in the parsley, salt, and lemon juice. Set aside.

- Pat salmon fillets dry and season with salt and pepper. Heat up a lightly oiled pan until very hot and place salmon skin side down. Depending on the thickness of your salmon, cook for about 4-6 minutes.

- Flip the salmon and add butter to the pan and when melted, baste the salmon for a few minutes. Slice into the thickest part of the salmon. It should still be a little rare inside. Serve salmon over a bed of frisée. Add a dollop of your almond pesto to the top, followed by some sliced shallots and slivered almonds.

Desserts

Banana Pudding

Ingredients:

• ½ cup heavy cream or ¼ cup heavy and ¼ cup almond milk

• 1 large egg yolk

• 3 tablespoon powdered erythritol

• ½ teaspoon xanthan gum

• ½ teaspoon banana extract

Directions:

• Combine the egg yolk, heavy cream (or almond milk and heavy cream), and powdered erythritol.

• In a double boiler, whisk constantly until the mixture thickens and the erythritol dissolves.

• Add the xanthan gum and whisk until thickened even more. The mixture should coat the back of a spoon.

• Add the banana extract and a pinch of salt, stir well.

• Strain through a sieve and transfer to the serving dish, cover with a wrap so that it touches the surface of the pudding.

• Refrigerate for about 4 hours and enjoy!

Double Chocolate Mousse

Ingredients:

- 1 oz. chocolate chips

- 1 cup heavy cream

- 4 oz. cream cheese

- ¼ cup powdered erythritol

- 2 tablespoon cocoa powder

Directions:

- Melt the chocolate chips at a very low heat in a pan with ¼ cup of heavy cream.

- In a bowl, beat the cream cheese and erythritol. Note: if you don't have powdered erythritol, simply pulse some granular erythritol in a food processor or blender until it's fine and powdery.

- Then, add in the melted chocolate chips, cocoa powder, and a pinch of salt. Beat well.

- In another bowl, beat the remaining ¾ cup of heavy cream until whipped.

- Into 2 cups or serving bowls, layer chocolate, cream, and top with chocolate chips and chocolate shavings.

Strawberry Pistachio Creamsicles

Ingredients:

- 8 oz. strawberries

- 2 oz. salted pistachios

- ½ cup heavy cream

- ½ cup almond milk

- 2 doonks stevia

Directions:

- Place your popsicle molds in the freezer beforehand. This will help accelerate the freezing process.

- Blend the strawberries, stevia, heavy cream, and almond milk until fully combined. Let this blend for about a minute so the cream has a chance to aerate and whip.

- Throw your pistachios into the mix and stir, do not blend! You can also use walnuts, cashews, or pecans.

- Pour the creamsicle mix into your cold popsicle molds and insert the bases. Freeze for about 2 hours or until set.

- To remove the creamsicles, allow hot water to run against the outside of the popsicle molds. This will melt some of the ice cream that sticks the creamsicles to the molds. Then gently pull on the bases until your ice cream is out.

Avocado Chocolate Pudding

Ingredients:

- 1 avocado

- 2 ½ tablespoons raw cocoa powder

- $^1/_{16}$ teaspoon ground cayenne pepper

- 1 teaspoon Ceylon cinnamon

- 1 tablespoon coconut milk

- 1 tablespoon erythritol

- ½ teaspoon vanilla extract

- 1 pinch stevia

- 1 pinch pink Himalayan sea salt

Directions:

- Cut and pit an avocado and blend it in a food processor until smooth.

- Add in your cocoa powder, coconut milk, and vanilla extract. Blend until smooth.

- Add in your favorite sweetener, cinnamon, a bit of stevia, and ground cayenne pepper. Keep blending and scraping down the sides of the food processor to get all the chunks evenly combined.

- Serve with a sprinkle of coarse Himalayan pink sea salt for a flavorful crunch.

Homemade Sugar-Free Chocolate Chips

Ingredients:

- 1 low-carb chocolate bar recipe

- 1 silicone pot holder

Directions:

- Start off by making your low-carb chocolate bar recipe.

- Pour the chocolate bar batter into the silicone pot holder.

- Using a spatula, spread the batter out into the little cavities.

- Place the silicone potholder in the freezer and freeze for about 1-2 hours.

- When they're frozen, twist the silicone molds and pop the chocolate chips out into a shallow plate.

- Use whenever a recipe calls for chocolate chips.

Enjoy!

Low-Carb Caramel

Ingredients:

- 4 tablespoons unsalted butter

- 4 tablespoons heavy cream

- 1 tablespoon erythritol

- 1 pinch of salt

Directions:

- Melt the butter in a small pan and let it cook until golden brown. This will give the caramel a deeper flavor.

- Pour the heavy cream and stir until combined. Lower the heat and simmer for a minute.

- Add a sweetener of choice and use erythritol. Let it dissolve for a minute. Add a pinch of salt as well. If you would like to make salted caramel, add more salt.

- Let it cook until you see it getting thicker and stickier.

- If your butter and cream are separating, you can pour the mixture into a NutriBullet and blend them to help them combine.

- Pour the caramel into a container, preferably glass, and continue to stir while it cools and thickens more to ensure your sauce is not too layered.

- To use right away, pour over the dessert of choice. You may also refrigerate the caramel for future use, but it will harden and it needs to be softened to be pourable or dippable.

Conclusion

With our intermittent fasting approach as a couple, we were able to conceive naturally and have our first child. With that fact alone, intermittent fasting has changed my life forever and made me the happiest that I could ever be. I am extremely grateful for having discovered what is known as intermittent fasting. With so much access to the internet, there was tons of information to educate me on this lifestyle approach. This information guided me in so many ways and assisted me with changing my eating habits to fit my lifestyle, while also making it the best life ever.

P.S. Thanks for reading! If you enjoyed this book, please consider leaving a short review on Amazon.

Made in United States
North Haven, CT
14 June 2024

53642723R00076